The Caste System
in
Terai Madhesh

THE CASTE SYSTEM IN TERAI MADHESH

Ram Dayal Rakesh

Adroit Publishers
New Delhi

Published by

ADROIT PUBLISHERS

4675/21, Ganpati Bhawan, Ansari Road,
Daryaganj, New Delhi-110 002

Phone : 011-23266030

Distributors

AKHIL BOOK DISTRIBUTORS

email: akhilbooks@yahoo.com
akhilbks@gmail.com

ISBN : 978-81-87393-10-8

Printed in India on behalf of M/s Adroit Publishers by
Akhil Sharma, E-mail: adroitpublishers@gmail.com

Contents

Introduction

Although the caste system was officially abolished in 1963 and a new civil code, the Mulki Ain, was promulgated in 1964 (slightly modified in 1975) this system is still prevalent in the Madheshi society. The Madheshi society is markedly and mainly rural in character. It is a highly complex society which is very difficult for doing a systematic and scientific study because there has been no systematic and scientific study done about it. It is very heterogeneous and its society and culture extremely diverse. Madheshi Society is unequivocally South Asian in its origin and genesis. It has been derived from the cultures of the Gangetic plains, with occasional links with North India. We all know that there is open border between Nepal and India. There is similarity between the two cultures. We share more or less the same cultural heritage. Madhesh is a race which depends on a common, but diverse culture and society. There are no noticeable differences in social organization, marriage patterns, linguistic dialects, and ritual performances. They also have in common some fundamental principles of social relations and cultural affinity. They have similar caste hierarchy. In India there was forward and backward class in ancient times but now she has forward castes such as Brahmin, Bhumihar, Rajput and Kayastha and in Backward Castes, Scheduled Castes, Scheduled Tribes and Dalits. In Nepal there are Brahmins, Chhetris, Rajputs, Kayasthas and Bhumihars in upper castes and in lower castes there are (O.B.C.) indigenous nationalities and Dalits. So there is clear cut caste hierarchy in the Nepalese society. So is the case with the Madheshi society. Madheshi society is still composite and complex and closed. Here I would like to quote:

> "The ideas behind hierarchy, purity and pollution, the conceptualization of gender inequality, the stress on communality, all symbolically meaningful factors, convey meaning to the actions undertaken by social agents and to the mechanisms enforcing social relations. "(Gerard Toffin 2008, P. 410).

> The Madheshi society has been divided into pure and impure castes. This division is the same and very similar to the one existing among the Nepali Parbatiya castes between pani chalne jat and pani nachalne jats, castes with whom water can be shared and those with whom it cannot. (Gerard Toffin 2008 P. 166.).

According to the 19th Century Mulki Ain, a distinction must be made between persons from whom water can not be accepted but contact with whom does not require purification by sprinkling of water, and those from whom water can be accepted and contact with whom does require purification by sprinkling (Macdonald 1975:282-285). The first category includes the Kalwar, Teli, Sudi. The second category includes Dom, Dushad, Halkhor, Chamar, Tatma, Khatwey etc.

These two categories of castes are clearly marked in the society. One category consists of Brahmins, Bhumihars, Rajputs, Kayasthas, Kanus, Halwais, Kumhars, Koiris (Kushwahas), Kurmis, Devs, Dhanuk, Sonar, Hajjam, Lohar, Dhobi, Rajdhob, Yadavas etc. with whom water can be shared and the other category consists of several castes such as Kalwar, Sudi, Teli etc, with whom water can not be shared. But now-a-days there is no such division seen apparently in the Madheshi society. Some years ago I was not allowed to take water alongwith Dhanuk castes of my village from the well because I belong to Kalwar caste which is considered untouchable. This was a very humiliating experience for me in the village. The caste system was so rigid that I could not break.

Foreign scholars have also the view of caste system in the Nepalese society. According to A. M. Hocart in the Hindu world people of low castes are considered to be Asura demons, in opposition to the high castes, who are collectively associated with the Deva Gods. One also finds a very strong relationship between, on the one hand, the low castes and the 'carnivorous' Goddesses, on the other hand, between the high castes and the masculine divinities, who are more often 'vegetarian'(at least in their pacified forms).

> There is caste system prevalent in the Hindu society from the very beginning. It is very difficult to trace out its origin. There is proof that it was in use in the period of the Rigveda. Indian scholar R.R. Diwakar has written in his book Bihar Through the Ages:
>
> "The caste system in its germinal form goes back to the Vedic age. The Aryans had already developed it to some extent by the time they reached Bihar. There were several classes in society, some of which were regarded as high, some as low. The cultivators, labours, massions, artisans potters, rash workers, fishermen and so on, were regarded as law." (p. 168).
>
> One another scholar is of this view that the caste system does not decide the position of the Hindus only; it decides the position of Non-Hindu in society. (Shridhar V. Ketkar. p. 20)

Dipankar Gupta argues that over-emphasis on any single hierarchy, whether Brahmin or Kshatriya, ignores the fact that there is no caste that is not proud of its legacy, beliefs and practices.

1

Definition of Caste

Tukaram a great saint poet has expressed displeasure about the caste system prevalent in the society in the following stanza. The Brahmin who flies into a rage at the touch of a Mahar that's no Brahmin. The only absolution for such Brahmin is to die for his own sin. He who refuses to touch a chandal has polluted mind says Tuka, a man *is only as caste as* his own belief.

Mahatma Gandhi was also against the casteism. His slogan was 'jat pat puchhe na koi, Hari ko bhaje so Hari ka hoi'. It can be translated freely as no body should ask about caste. He who remembers Lord Hari, belongs to Him.

The word caste is of Spanish and Portuguese origin. Caste means lineage or race. It is derived from the Latin word castus, which means pure. The Spaniards were the first to use, but its Indian application is from the Portuguese, who had so applied it in the middle of the fifteenth century. The current spelling of the word is after the French word 'caste' which appears in 1740 in the 'academics' and is hardly found before 1800. Before that time it was spelt as 'cast'. In the sense of race or breed of man it was used as early as 1555 A.D. The Spanish word 'casta' was applied to the mixed breed between Europeans, Indians Americans and Negroes. But 'caste' was not used in its Indian sense till the seventeenth century. The Indian use is the leading one now, and it has influenced all other uses. As the Indian idea of caste was but vaguely understood this word was loosely applied to the hereditary classes. Her manners had not that repose which stamps the caste of Vere de Vere. Tennyson's Lady Clara vere de vere of Europe resembling the castes of India, who keep themselves socially distinct (Shridhar v. ketkar).

Darwin has applied this word to different classes of social insects. The Portuguese used this word to denote the Indian institution, as they thought such a system was intended to keep purity of blood. The word caste was originally applied by the Portuguese in the sixteenth century, and since the Portuguese casta means 'pure ' or 'chaste', it suggests very well the importance to the Hindu of maintaining the ritual and social purity of each jati. I would like to quote here:

> 'When we refer to caste we are really speaking of Jati which means 'birth', and this is far more important for Hindus because it affects so many aspects of daily life. Where as there are only four classes in Hinduism there are thousands of castes. Caste is not a religious institution, unlike Varna, but is economic and geographical in origin, though it is impossible to say exactly why and how all the castes came out. ' (Jeaneane Fowler:Hinduism: 2000. P. 23.).

He has also shed light on the significance of each and every caste in the following lines:

> "Each Jati has its own special caste regulation in terms of food, occupation, marriage, social interaction and the like, and from each caste will come a number of sub-castes making the whole system a highly complicated one which defies examination. Castes may often be occupational but this does not preclude a member of one caste working at the occupation of another, for example in agriculture; this results in a very complex system. '(Jeaneane Fowler: Hinduism:2000. P.)

Definition of a caste by other writers- Definitions of caste can be found in the various volumes of the Report of the Census of India for 1901.

M. Senart has written in his book, after reminding his readers that no statement that can be made on the subject can be considered as absolutely true, that the apparent relations of the facts admit of numerous shades of distinction and that only the most general characteristics cover the whole of the subject, he goes on to describe a caste as a close corporation, in theory at any rate rigoriously hereditary equipped with a certain traditional and independent or organization including a chief and a council, meeting on occasion in assemblies of more or less plenary authority and joining together at certain festivals; bound together by common occupations, which relate more particularly to marriage and to food and to questions of ceremonial pollution, and ruling its members by the exercise of jurisdiction the extent of which varies, but which succeeds in making the authority of the community more felt by the sanction of certain penalties and above all by final irrevocable exclusion from the group.

Nesfield defines a caste as a "class of the community which disowns any connection with any other class and can neither intermarry nor eat nor drink with any but persons of their own community."

Sir H. Risley defines a caste as follows, "A caste may be defined as a collection of families or groups of families bearing a common name which usually denotes or is associated with specific occupation, claiming common descent from a mythical ancestor, human or divine, professing to follow the same professional callings and are regarded by those who are competent to give an opinion as forming a single homogenous community.

Shridhar V. Ketkar has defined caste in the following words:

"A caste is a social group having two characteristics.

1. Membership is confined to those who are born of members and includes all persons so born.
2. The members are forbidden by an inexorable social law to marry outside the group. Each one of such groups has a special name by which it is called. Several of such small aggregates are grouped together under a common name, while these larger groups are but subdivisions of groups still larger which have independent names.

Thus it is clear that larger group is called caste where as smaller group is called subcaste. When we talk of Maithil Brahmin and Kanyakuj and kantah, the first one would be called a caste where as the latter would be called a subcaste but in a general way both of them might be called castes. Likewise kalwar caste has four groups: Viahut kalwar, Jaiswal, Jaiswar and Kharidaha and Kalal. Though Kalal's traditional calling is the distillation of liquor, all of them are no longer engaged in that now.

Teli is also of two kinds- Magahiya and Kanaujiya. Yadav has also two kinds- Majhraut and Kishnaut.

"These divisions and subdivision are introduced on different principles. In this way two hundred million Hindus are so much divided and sub divided that there are castes who can not marry outside fifteen families. On the other hand there are some castes in which the process of division and subdivision has not been carried to its logical extent which can boast of five millions. These three thousand castes with their subcastes put together make Hindu society. There is no intermarriage and very little of social inter course in its proper sense.

The internal structure of a caste is very complex. According to B.R. Ambedkar caste is not a physical object like a wall of bricks or a line of barbed wire which prevents the Hindus from commingling and which has, therefore, to be pulled down. Caste is a notion, it is a state of the mind. The destruction of caste does not therefore mean the destruction of a physical barrier. It means a national change." He further adds that caste is not a division of labour, it is a division of labourers.

Caste composition: Sushil K. Naidu has made a survey of Hindu castes and written in his book, Nepal: Society and Culture in the following lines:

> "The Hindu households consists of 22 castes. Since many of them are not found in significant numbers and the number of castes are too large for comparision. Castes have been grouped into five categories on the basis of the homonencity in the pattern of living as well as their relative positions in the society. Muslim is not a caste but a distinct

community. The castes in hierarchy in the Terai villages have been classified as under:

Upper Castes: Brahmin, Chhetri, Rajput, Giri.

Middle Castes: Ahir, Koeri, Kurmi, Barayee.

Business Castes: Baniya, Kalwar, Kanu, Teli, Sonar.

Functional Castes: Lohar, Mallah, Konhar, Gond, Nonia, Nai.

Harijan: Tatma, Dhobi, Dusadh, Chamar.

Prevalent Hindu castes of Terai/ Madhesh are listed here grouped roughly indescending order of ritual status position:

Brahman Hajam	Kalwar	
Bhumihar	Mali	Dhobi
Rajput	Barai	Halkhor
Kayastha	Halwai	Dom
Nunia	Mallah	Dhusadh
Kurmi	Badhai	Chamar
Kewat	Lohar	Tatma
Gwala	Teli	Khatwe.

Though the nomenclature Harijan is not in use in Nepal, it has been retained here for convenience in identification of caste status. (Sushil K. Naidu: 1994 P. 203.)

Hindus are very deeply religious minded since the time immemorial. They believe in many Gods and Goddesses and pray them in morning and evening regularly. They make temples for them so that they can pray and recite religious scriptures to pacify themselves whenever they are desperate and disappointed. By doing this they perform religious activites in their daily life. I would like to quote here "Hindus observe caste not because they are inhuman or wrong headed". Ambedkar wrote in 1936. They observe caste because they are deeply religious.

Another scholar has this view about Hinduism:-

> "Hinduism has no orthodoxy but only orthopraxy (correct practice). Many Hindus for example are united by the rituals of coconuts and camphor. Some Hindus break coconuts to symbolize the offerings of one's head to the deities.

Likewise, they light camphor to wave before the temple deity as the medium through which their offerings are carried to the Gods. Hinduism has been defined in the right context in the following lines: "In books on the world's religions, Hinduism is readily defined, indeed much as the earlier orientalists defined it as a religion united intellectually by the age- old Vedas, socially by the four classes of castes (varnas) and spiritually by the laws of Dharma Karma which govern the transgration of souls. Frykenberg argues that this text book definition has been made to encompass everything from the philosophical and the ritual, features of the cosmic order in all its highest sophistication to the bloodiest, crudest, meanest and most savage practices of the most primitive peoples.

According to one Nepali anthropologist all the castes are followers of Hinduism:

> "All of the castes under discussion are strictly Hindu, although the degree of orthodoxy declines as one descends the hierarchy. They worship all the deities of the Hindu pantheon. Brahma, Vishnu, Mahadev, Gauri, Parvati, Lakshmi, Sarswati, Durga, Rama, Krishna, Ganesh, Bhimsen and so on. There are one or more temples in each village, and the Terai boasts two particularly holy places of pilgrimage the temples of Ram and Janaki at Janakpur in Dhanusha district, and the birthplace of Buddha at Lumbini in the district of Rupandehi.

Almost every family keeps a family deity called Gossain in the home near the hearth. They worship their gossain daily, offering special food during festivals and family ceremonies, and set aside one special day each year for a special gossain observance. The Gossain may be Durga, Bhairava, Devi or any other such Hindu deity. "Dor Bahadur Bista: People of Nepal: P. 117.

But due to modernization and globalization, caste in the society is loosing its grip in group.

> "The caste system is gradually being replaced by a class system. Modernization has both compelled and helped various ethnic and caste groups to participate in any profession (Rishi Keshav Raj Regmi 1999).

Another scholar has also marked this change in the caste system in the following lines:

> "The extent and nature of changes in the institution of caste are certainly different between the urban and rural areas. The decline of caste as a system is more perceptible in cities than in rural areas, where as the growth of castes as articulated interest groups is more noticeable in urban areas. This should not be construed to mean that there is no semblance of a caste system in cities, and that the mobilization of people on caste lines is absent in villages. "N. Jayaram 1996.

One another scholar has opposed the hegemony of Hinduism which has been in vogue for last so many centuries. He may be right to some extent today because of the effect of modernization and globalization. The caste system is changing very rapidly these days. No educated person is in favour of it because it has become obsolute . He has also asserted and accepted that there is caste discrimination in the society. He is of this opinion:

> "Despite the oppression created by the Hindu caste system, one can not justify exclusive rights of any caste/ ethnicity as part of a historical solution. " (Suman Khadka: TKP. Nov. 6. 2012)

There is caste discrimination in Nepal and it is only because of the superiority of some upper castes people who consider themselves superior than others by birth but this is not justifiable. I would like to quote here:

> "One can not deny that caste-based discrimination has remained in Nepal despite legal equality. This is due to weak enforcement by the state and prevailing customary rules over formal constitutional rules. " (Suman Khadka:TKP. Nov. 6. 2012)

Karanth finds that caste in rural India is not a static phenomenon and is characterized by mobility. Further, Sanskritization is an integral part of mobility, and this is true of the SCs as well. He also notes the familiar phenomenon of castes claiming to be high in a traditional context, and 'backward' in the context of the struggle for getting access to education and government job (M. N. Shriniwas 1996).

The whole society has been divided into 'touchables and untouchables. One Indian scholar has this opinion about the caste system:

> "Caste system has been an important determining factor in dividing the contemporary Hindu society. The whole society has been divided into touchables and untouchables. Under the caste system, traditional occupation, *commonality* rules and ritual purity are regarded important. " Prakash Upadhya: Nepali Culture and Society. P. 280.

Jung Bahadur Rana has categorised castes of Nepal into following groups:

1. Tagadharis: Who wear sacred thread and consider themselves as twice born.
2. Matawalis: Who drink liquor frequently.
3. Pani na chalne chhoi chhito halnuparne: Castes from whom water can't be accepted, but whose touch does not require purification of the sprinkling of water.
4. Pani na chalne choi chhito halnuparne: Which means Untouchable castes.

But this stratification of caste does not apply in Terai-Madhesh. The caste system of Terai-Madhesh is the same and similar of Indian states of Bihar, U.P. and Bengal. There is caste hierarchy in the Hindu society, there is no doubt in it. One scholar has opined about this in the following lines:

> Against the' hierarchy' thesis Dipankar Gupta argues that over-emphasis on any single hierarchy, whether Brahmin or Kshatriya, ignores the fact that there is no caste that is not proud of its legacy, beliefs and practices. (Gaurang R. Sahay: Caste in Question: P. 115.)

2

Origin of the Caste System

The origin of the caste system is thought to have developed in South Asia towards the end of the Vedic Period. This was essentially a division of labour into four broad groups known as the Varna. It was hierarchical in nature with Brahmins at the top, engaged in philosophical and religious pursuits, Kshatriya (also known as Chettri), involved in military and political field. Vaishya, the businessmen and farmers, and Shudra, the lowest Varna, engaged in manual labor and traditional crafts. At first, there was some mobility between the major caste divisions, but later it became impossible, in principle, to change the caste status labelled from the birth(Robertson and Mishra, 1997).

The functions of each Jati were divided according to the intellectual capacity, physical fitness, economic drive and serviceability to the society. The members of one Jati were differenciated from others by the nature of work they adopted. This concept has been thus elaborated by lawgiver Manu. He transcendental, in order to protect his creation, assigned distinct duties to those born of mouth, arms, thighs and feet. Teaching and pursuing Vedic studies, offering sacrifices and guiding those who wished to sacrifice gifts, these were assigned by him to the Brahmin.

There is caste system not in India and Nepal only but in the whole world. One scholar has opined rightly in the following lines:

> "Caste has been an important element in enhancing stratification not only in the Nepalese context, but also in the world context, although

the caste based stratification of the remaining world is racial. The racial stratification between Blacks and Whites of America is comparable to the caste-based stratification of Nepal & India. Aryans, who had migrated from Middle -East and who had settled in the plains of the Ganges, were the initiators of caste system. " Prakash Upadhaya:Nepali Culture and Society: P. 122-123.

Leela Dube has right opinion about caste. She has expressed her view in the following lines:

> "A Jati or caste has a distinctive culture, a certain commonality that imparts a sense of identity to its members. These cultural practices in turn are learnt largely within the family and kinship networks. Modes of worship, fasts and festivals, rules governing concerns of purity and pollution, and the organization of space, constitute interrelated and intermeshed elements which impart commonality and identity to members of a caste. "(Leela Dube 1996)

Sociologists are of this view today that stereotype caste system has been challenged and changed to a great extent. I would like to quote here:

> "Sociologists have now effectively challenged the stereotype about the caste system being a closed and rigid system and not allowing individuals to give up their hereditary occupation and take up new occupations. "(M. N. Panini 1996).

Sociologists, beginning with G. S. Ghurye, have highlighted the inherent flexibilities in the system. Ghurye (1961:241-281) pointed out that certain occupations and tasks such as cultivation (except touching of the plough which was prohibited for the Brahmins), administration and military services were open to all castes.

Caste system has existed in the village level. It has been abolished in urban areas not legally but socially. There is no caste system and caste hierarachy felt in city areas in any hotel and restaurant. This has become fact now a days. One scholar has noted it down in the following lines:

> "It must be pointed out, however, that caste as a system has existed only locally, i.e., in a single village or a few linked villages. "(N. Jayaram 1996).

The caste system is in vogue in India and Nepal only. There is caste hierarchy in all the states of India and it is not so easy to abolish it in near future. There are scheduled castes and scheduled tribes in India. There are Dalits also. Likewise there is strong caste system in Nepal also. One scholar has this view:

> "I shall now make a tentative remarks about caste in rural India. In the first place, it may not be appropriate any more to refer to caste in rural India as a 'system'. Castes exist as individual groups, but no longer integrated into a system, with the dovetailing of their interests. Castes are in competition with each other for obtaining access to material resources, education and a share in political power. "(G.K. Karanth 1996)

Another scholar has the same view about the caste system. I would like to quote here:

> "It is a matter of common knowledge that caste plays an active role in the political life of the country at all levels. Indeed allotment of party tickets, formation of state ministries, and appointment to numerous boards, committees and commissions, are made on a caste basis, and this seems to be accepted as legitimate by the bulk of the people. "(G. K. Karanth 1996)

There has been drastic change in the caste system now a days. It has been modernized in many senses. There are many reasons of it. One scholar has pointed out these reasons in the following manners. Allow me to quote:

> "Universal adult franchise. Greater political awareness among the weaker sections and better opportunities of employment and mobility are all responsible for the changed situation. "(G.K. Karanth 1996.)

The Mandal Commission in India was also against of caste system. I would like to quote here:

> "The Mandal Commission argued that in India the caste system was the root cause of structural inequality. It had therefore no inhibition against recognizing caste as the main factor in the backwardness of the O.B.Cs. The members of the commission considered that this social category was made of castes- mostly of low ritual status. "(Religion, Caste and Politics in India. P. 494).

3

Evolution of the Caste System

It is well known fact that the caste system has been evolved from the very ancient time. It has been evolved from such Hindu scriptures and law books as the Bhagavad Gita and the Dharmashastra. Both the cognitive categories of Jatis (large scale endogamous descent groups) and varnas(ranked classification of Jatis) on the one hand, and the associated concepts of Jatidharma and Varnadharma (the religiously-ordained duties for the Jati and Varna members) on the other, were defined and interpreted in terms of the theological doctrines of Hinduism. (N. Jayaram 1996).

So this is clear that the Caste system and Hinduism is interwined and interlinked to each other.

According to one recent research finding also it is confirmed in the following lines:

> 'Though Nepali society is regarded as multi-ethnic, multi-religious, multi-cultural and multilingual, the feadualistic Hindu caste system still maintains the deep division among various caste groups. The caste system which has its roots in the ancient religious texts, codes and traditions derived from them, was formalized by the 1854 Civil Code. Although it was legally abolished by an amendment of the Civil Code in 1963, the caste system, including untouchability, is still rampant in the Nepali society." (Ranjit Kanaujiya, the Republica daily. April, 12, 2013).

In Hindu society there are hundreds of castes. So there is strong caste system in it. There is not only caste system in Hindus but in non- Hindus also. I would like to quote here.

"The caste system does not decide the position of the Hindus only; it decides the position of Non-Hindus in society, e.g. the Mohammedans and Christians have a certain definite status according to Hindu social theory (Shreedhar V. Ketkar 1909)

Another scholar Nesfield has also defined caste in the following lines:

"a class of the community which disowns any connection with any other class and can neither inter marry nor eat or drink with any but persons of their own community. Another scholar Sir H. Risley has another definition for caste. Allow me to quote here:

"A caste may be defined as a collection of families or group of families bearing a common name which usually denotes or is associated with specific occupation claiming common descent from a mythical ancestor, human or divine professing to follow the same professional callings and are regarded by those who are competent to give an opinion as forming a single homogenous community."

Yet another scholar A. L. Kroeber (1931) has defined caste as a caste may be defined as an endogamous and hereditary subdivision of an ethnic unit occupying a position of superior or inferior rank of social system in comparison with other subdivision."

One scholar has defined caste in the following lines:

"Caste is a system in which an individual's rank and its accompanying rights and obligations are ascribed on the basis of birth into a particular group. "(William Writer)

Mr. E.A.M. Blunt defines caste as follows:

"An endogamous or a collection of endogamous groups, bearing a common name, membership of which is hereditary, imposing on the members certain restriction in the matter of social intercourse; either following a common traditional occupation of claiming a common origin; and generally regarded as forming a single homogeneous community."

According to Majumdar and Madan, " A caste is a closed class."

C.H. Cooley, "When a class is somewhat strictly hereditary and whose contacts are restricted accordingly."

According to Lundbert Writer, "A caste is a social category whose members are assigned a permanent status within a social hierarchy and whose contacts are restricted accordingly."

A. W. Green defines caste in the following lines:

> "Caste is a system of stratification in which mobility up and down in the status ladder, at least ideally may not occur."

According to Anderson and Parker,

> "Caste is that extreme form of social class organization in which the position of individual in the status hierarchy is determined by crescent and birth."

The origin of the caste is still lost in oblivion. There is no evidence when the caste was born. Its future is also not clear. A writer and public intellectual from Tamil Nadu Ravikumar's opinion is given here.

> "In the caste of caste, no two people agree on when exactly it was born inspite of the rigorous research that has gone into it, everybody is unsure about where this miraculous birth took place. Since origin and history cannot be pushed aside, it is crucial that a birth certificate for caste be obtained as soon as possible for us to predict its future."

According to one another scholar there is genetic purity in the caste system. It is fully maintained in it. A genetically pure line is maintained due to the caste endogamy and class exogamy practiced in the caste system.

Shridhar V. Ketkar's observation is quotable here.

> "There are two important elements in the Hindu caste system; for example, endogamy and hierarchy. The classes, races, and occupations exclude themselves from other groups while there is an understanding that one group is superior to the other. of these two let endogamy be singled for consideration." 1909.

> "Keeping the blood pure is a must in the caste system. This feeling is coupled with the desire for keeping the blood pure when the

> pretensions of this upper layer sufficiently increase. " (Shreedhar V. Ketkar 1901)

The caste system is the product of Aryan civilization. The role of Arya is very significant in assimilating the different castes which were in vogue. The Aryan people brought different castes in the main stream. It is also true that there were Dravids, and Negroes before Aryan came in the Indian subcontinent.

Another scholar has also more or less the same view:

> "Caste is generally held, and rightly so, as having received its rigid form in the Post-rigvedic period. There were only three types of professional categories of the Rigvedic Aryans known as Brahma, Kshatra and Vis. The great bulk of indigenous population was called by them with different names: Dasa, Asura and Mleccha. As time went on, these three professional groups assumed a rigid shape by getting fixed on a hereditary line. There are definite traces of the four stereotyped caste groups in the later phase of Vedic literature. " K. C. Mishra: Tribes in the Mahabharat: P. 319

The Purusa Sukta in Rigveda (X90. 12) names four castes for the first time. The Yajurveda (Vaja. Samhita, 30) names a lot of occupations. But there is hardly any evidence to recognize them as castes or subcastes in the later sense.

There is a hymn which tells of the sacrifice of a huge primeval man called Purus from whom the four classes came.

> When they divided man
> Into how many parts did they divide him?
> What was his mouth? what his warms?
> What are his thighs called? what his feet?
> The Brahman was his mouth
> The arms were made the Prince
> His thighs the common people
> And from his feet the serf was born.

The following four castes have been mentioned in the Yajurveda Samhita.

1. The Brahmins-who devoted themselves to learning, acquiring and giving wisdom to the other three classes. Brahmins are traditionally priests.

According to one scholar:

> "The Brahmin was never an economically self-supported class and only a few Brahmins could exercise some influence in the administration or actual public life. "He further explains that the orthodox view of the supremacy of Brahamin caste reveals one positive fact, that the Brahmins formed the most homogenous group or had racially been the purest of all castes in ancient India. K. C. Mishra:Tribes in the Mahabharat:P. 328

2. The Kshatriyas-who devoted themselves to the theory and practice of war and to whom the government of the people was entrusted.

The actual caste system began from Kshatriya according to K.C. Mishra. I would like to quote him here:

> "On the other hand, it is from the Kshatriya class itself that actual caste system or the segregation of so many subcaste groups received impetus in subsequent days of decline of tribal culture. " K.C. Mishra :Tribes in the Mahabharat: P. 329.

> "The Rajputs claim to be the direct descents of the Kshstriyas. This is not acknowledged in particular localities. They are in general a proud race. There are many destinations among them based mostly on the region to which they belong. There are a number of clans among them, quite a few of which are found in Bihar. A good many of the Rajputs are cultivators, thekedars and Zamindars. Many of them have taken to trade, or sought service in the army, or the police, or as gatekeepers. There are many others claiming Kshatriyahood. " R. R. Diwakar: Bihar Through the Ages. P. 694.

> The higher castes, especially, Rajputs, enforce very strict discipline upon their womenfolk. A woman would never appear without covering her face before men who are senior to her husband, or before other outsiders. A Rajput never marries a person related through common descent but two brothers or cousins can bring in wives from the same family." Dor Bahadur Bist: People of Nepal: P. 115.

A Rajput never marries a person related through common descent, but two brothers or two cousins can bring in wives from the same family. A widower can marry the youngest of his diseased wife.

Thus, the Rajputs were at once rulers, warriors and landowners, and it would be impossible to choose a single occupation by which to designate them.

The higher castes-Brahmins, Bhumihars, Rajputs and Kayasths do not practice widow re-marriage nor do they ever recognize the second marriage of any woman. Lower castes, on the other hand, practice second marriages for widows. R. R. Diwakar: Bihar Through the Ages: P. 694

3. Vaishyas- Who devoted themselves to trade and agriculture.
4. Sudras- Who helped and served the other three classes.

All of the castes under discussion are strictly Hindu although the degree of orthodoxy declines as one descends the heiarachy. They worship all the deities of the Hindu pantheon. Brahma, Vishnu, Mahadev, Gauri, Parvati, Lakshmi, Sarswati, Durga, Rama, Krishna, Ganesh, Bhimsen, and so on. There are one or more temples in each village, and the Terai boasts two particularly holy places of pilgrims-the temples of Ram and Janaki at Janakpur in Dhanusha district, and the birthplace of Buddha at Lumbini in the district of Rupandehi. Almost every family keeps a family deity called Gossai in the home near the hearth. They worship their Gosai daily, offering special food during festivals and family ceremonies, and set aside one special day each year for a special gossai observance. The Gosai may be Durga, Bhayval, Devi, or any other such deity.

One scholar has highlighted the qualities of different castes in the following lines:

> "The functions of each jati were divided according to the intellectual capacity, physical fitness, economic drive and serviceality to the society. The members of one jati were differenciated from others by the nature of work they adopted. This concept has been thus elaborated by lawgiver Manu:

> "He transcendental, in order to protect his creation, assigned distinct duties to those of mouth, arms thighs and feet:

Teaching and pursuing Vedic studies, offering sacrifices and guiding those who wished to sacrfice gifts, those were assigned by him to the Brahmin.

Protection of the peoples, gifts, sacrifices, study of the Vedas, non-attachment from the objects of the senses, these were ascribed to the Khashtriyas.

The Shudras were assigned only one duty, service of other castes without the feeling of being subordinated. Manusmiriti, 1, 87-91.

Caste-system: Background

"The institution of caste occupies an important place in the social organization of India. It has come to be bound the Hindu religion and has pervaded many of the social conceptions of the Hindus and the codes of the then Hindu law-givers. Many European and Indian scholars have described it as a unique institution peculiar to India. No uniform or consistent account of the origin of the castes can be gathered from the Hindu sacred books."

One scholar has this type of view that in the beginning the institution of caste has no concern and connection with birth. I would like to quote here:

> "In the beginning caste had nothing to do with birth and was merely a distinction based upon qualities, character and occupation. But there can be no doubt that whatever the reasons for the origin of the system, castes soon became hereditary and more or less rigid. He has further elaborated it in the following lines:

> "In the Mahabharat Yudhisthira says that Sudras possessing the qualities and virtues of a Brahmin should be treated as Brahmin and vice versa. In the Dharmavyadha episode of the Mahabharat, a Brahmin was advised by a Brahmin lady to seek knowledge of Dharma (righteousness) from a butcher, which he accepted that and also took food and water at the hands of his teacher."

He has further stated that there were main four castes in the beginning. According to his version Aryan tribe has the following divisions;

> "There are traces of the division of the Aryan tribe into the'holy power (Brahmin), the kingly power (Kstra/Kshatriya) and the commonalty (Vaish/Vaishya), and the caste system was only in process of development in the Rigvedic times. The kingship and priesthood was hereditary and two words= (Varna and Jati) used by Sanskrit writers in one and the same sense. Varna indicated colour which means race."

According to the Yajurveda Samhita there are the following four classes:

1. The Brahmins-who devoted themselves to learning, acquiring and giving wisdom to the other three classes. It should not be confused with Brahmin (the Supreme Soul) One Great God or Ishwara.
2. The Kshatriyas: who devoted themselves to the theory and practice of war and to whom the government of the people was entrusted.
3. Vaishyas: who devoted themselves to trade and agriculture.
4. Sudras: who helped and served the other three classes. Tulsi Das has forcasted the future of Shudras in Kalijug (Iron age) like this:

> "Sudra karahi jap tap vrata nana. Baithi Barasan kahahi purana. "

This can be translated as this:

> "Shudras, on the other hand, indulge in all sorts of prayers and penances and vow and expound the Puranas from exalted seat.

The Hindu caste system is mainly based on the principles of purity and pollution which is still present some how or other till today. This has divided the Hindu society in so many ways. Some people like it and some people do not like it. The Mulki Ain has also abolished this caste system long before but it is still in vogue in the society. Upendra Yadav has also admitted this fact in the following lines:

> "Caste- based hierarchical discrimination, exploitation and superstition had been the fate of average Nepalese people. "(Upendra Yadav 2005, P. 4)

The Hindu caste system is based on the principles of purity and pollution, has led to the creation of a highly stratified society with unequal and hierarchical assignments of economic and civil rights ascribed by birth. While endogamy and social separation have caused intence group inequalities to perpetuate, practices of untouchability and caste based discrimination have ensured the exclusion of members of the so-called 'low castes' from preferred positions of the society. In addition to being denied educational, civil, cultural, religious and occupational rights, the Scheduled Castes (erstwhile untouchables) had to suffer under the deleterious effects of residential and social segregation (Debipriya Chatterjee 2012). Debipriya Chatterjee presented a paper on 'Can affirmative action policies succeed in the presence of social marginalization? In a seminar held in Kathmandu, July 18-20, 2012. I personally agree cent percent with her view. So I am quoting her in the following lines:

> Although the caste system has its root in Hinduism, it is interesting to note that other 'egalitarian' religions, like Islam and Christianity, as practiced in South Asia have developed their own notions of caste-like hierarchy. The caste system, by its very construction has both the dimensions of discrimination and segregation as integral to its very existence. Consequently, it would be wishful thinking that the biases that are so deeply ingrained from these centuries-old practices would be replaced within a couple of generations in modern times. A more pragmatic approach would be to recognize that dıscrımınatıon and segregation would continue to actively engage in public policy to counter the deleterious effects of the caste system. (Debipriya Chatterjee 2012).

The caste system is very complex and complicated in Hinduism. I would like to quote here:

> "The most complex phenomenon of the practiced Hinduism is its caste system. Caste comprises endogamous group of people, speaking a common language and having common social customs and religious beliefs or practices; this last aspect only at the micro level, such as having own priests for ceremonies like marriages.

> Where a caste group is large it has a number of small groups which are subcastes. In such a situation, endogamy is the norm only within the subcaste. Even mutual social intercourse and common or community feeding or drinking, or smoking, is permitted within the members of the sub-caste only. The sub-caste has an identity of its own, and has a graded position within the caste structure, which structure has a graded position within the overall Hindu Hierarchy. " (Jagdish Singh:Growth of Hindu Religion and Culture: P. 243.).

In his book Caste and Class in India: G.S. Ghure has observed that to get a sociologically correct idea of the caste system, it is the sub-caste which needs to be recognized as the basis or foundation unit upon which the system rests.

> "Yet, when it comes to marriage, it is the caste and not the race that will decide the issue. " (Jagdish Singh: Growth of Hindu Religion and Culture: P. 244).

There is a good treatise on castes and subcastes in his book which needs to be mentioned here.

In the caste system there are at least two hundred groups which can be and are called castes, with distinct caste names. The number of subcastes which are endogamous, is around two thousand. One feature of the caste was a common priesthood. The castes sometimes lie scattered over a number of villages performing the function of their stations, like the village cobbler, the blacksmith the carpenter. Sometimes they are in the communities, like weavers. A number of factors combine to decide the caste of a person, and the most important is his possesion.

A Brahmin's function is to perform religious jobs, and promote education. A vani, a Baniya is a trader. He supplies consumer items to the people of the village, and also take care of the sale and purchase of the surplus agriculture produce.

Kashatriyas, who have any number of castes and subcastes within their varna, are the people who compose the military; kings gave them large tracts of land where they could train and maintain contingents for war. Brahmin had the top position amongst the castes since he was the teacher, Guru, preceptor, a religious guide; he helped people to establish communion with God. The Khastriya came the next, for he was the ruler and safeguarded the integrity of the caste. Vaisyas, the Vanis, came the next, and the last place went to the Shudras, who comprised the workforce, the labourers, the artisans, the people who served the other three *varnas.* A large number of castes in the case of the Shudras went by the name of the profession they followed, like *Lohar Backsmith, Tarkhan Carpenter,* and so on.

Our country Nepal is a multi-racial, multi-cultural, multi-lingual and multi-religious in many respects. There are numerous ethnic groups and they all have their own languages and cultures.

According to one scholar:

> "Nepalese society is a multi-ethnic, multi-religious and multicultural country. Diversity exists in every walks of Nepalese life. This diversity has been mere intensified by the prevailing caste system in Nepal. Caste is an ascribed status and under it the status of an individual is determined not by his achievements, but by the quality of his birth. As caste is an ascribed status, the qualities of a person belonging to the lower caste is rejected because there exists no regards to the lower caste is rejected because there exists no regards for the qualifications of a lower caste man under the dogma of the caste system. " Prakash Upadhaya:Nepali culture and Society: P. 133.

> "Nepal is a multiethnic, multi-religious, and multi-lingual country. This diversity has, however, posed problems for Nepal because the rulers of the country have in the past either favoured or excluded particular groups on the basis of ethnicity, religion, language, etc. , thereby creating wide socio-economic disparities amongst different groups. Despite its overwhelming cultural diversity, until recently Nepal remained a predominantly 'Hindu kingdom with a Hindu polity, though not necessarily a Hindu society' through deliberate state policies." (Pradhan, R. 2002 in State of Nepal. P. 5).

The Interim Constitution of Nepal recognises for the first time in Nepalese history the cultural diversity of Nepal, stating it to be a 'multi-caste, multi-lingual, multi-religious, multi-cultural and multi-ideological nation.'

One Nepali scholar has also the same and similar view about the cultural and linguistic diversity of Nepal in the following lines:

> "The remarkable linguistic and social diversity in the Tarai can also pose a problem for the consolidation of a pan-Madhesi identity. Madhesis speak Maithili, Bhojpuri, and Awadhi that are also spoken across the border in India. On the other hand, ethnic groups such as the Tharus, Rajbanshi, Dhimal, and Gangai have their own languages. Similarly, the whole spectrum of the caste-based hierarchy is to be found amongst the Hindu Madhesis. Brahmins and Kshatriya groups are situated at the top, while the Dalits at the bottom are considered impure and untouchables. There is also a substantial presence of the' middle castes', like the Yadavas, Suris, and Kurmis. Caste divisions govern social relations and play a significant role in forming political choices. Very often they also shape economic stratification. (Hari Prasad Bhattarai: Recognising Diversity: P. 160).
>
> Mishra, C. (2003), has appropriately indicated three important factors that contibuted to local isolation and involution and, thus, to the emergence and rise of multiple cultures in Nepal. (Notes on Pluralism in Nepal, Chumlung Bulletin, Vol. 2, No. 3).

The Interim Constitution of Nepal 2006 defines Nepal as a 'state which is secular, inclusive and democratic and guarantees equal and social justice.

At present , one hundred and twenty five ethnic and caste groups and sub-groups, and more than one hundred languages have been documented according to the census of 2011. In addition, these caste, ethnic, ethnic, and language groups are further divided into eight major religious groups: Hindu, Buddhist, Islam, Kirat, Jain, Sikh, Christian, and Bahai. Broadly speaking, the following categories of people are to be found:

1. Pahadis: Hill and mountain groups considered caste Hindus (twice born, ascetic castes as well as so called'untouchables') with Nepali as their mother tounge, comprise about 39 percent of the population.
2. Janajatis: Tibeto-Burman language-speaking hill and mountain ethnic groups comprise about 22 percent.

3. Newars: consisting of Hindus and Buddhists of different castes, comprise about five percent.

4. Madheshis: People who trace their origin to the plains comprise 32 percent. Among them about 18 percent are caste Hindus; about 10 percent are Janjatis (ethnic groups of the plains); about 4 percent Muslims; and a few other groups. An attempt has been made to define Madheshi in the following lines:

> "Madhesis are defined as non-Pahadi people who, regardless of their place of birth or residence, speak a mother tongue that belongs to the plains. However, in contemporary discourse, the category does not encompass the lowland and indigenous ethnic groups and the Muslims. Indigenous peoples like Tharus, Rajbanshis, Gangai, and Dhimals, and Muslims have claimed that they have their own independent identity that is different from that of the Madhesis. Some groups, particularly Tharus, Dhimals, and Gangais, claimed that they are the original inhabitants of the Tarai and that the Madhesis are later migrants."

But it is wrong to say that Madhesis are migrants. They are also original inhabitants of Tarai/Madhesh from time immemorial.

5. Others: Marwaris, Bengalis, Sikhs, Christians, and the 'Others' category of the census add up to about 2 persent.

Thus it is right to say and support the following statement made by two eminent scholars:

> The Nepali people are, in essence, a cultural mosaic compromising different caste and ethnic groups belonging to the Tibeto-Burman and Indo-Aryan linguistic families. This is indicative of the waves of migrations that have occurred over two thousand years from the north and south. Although different groups have mingled with each other, they differ widely in cultural terms and have also adapted differently. Their sense of being different from each other, also seems to have persisted throughout history. (Pradhan, R. and A. shrestha 2005).

According to T.R.Vaidya and B.R. Bajracharya the remarkable linguistic and social diversity in the Tarai can also pose a problem for the consolidation of a pan-Madhesi identity. Madhesis speak Maithili, Bhojpuri, and Awadhi that are also spoken across the border in India. On the other hand, ethnic groups such as the Tharus, Rajbanshi, Dhimal, and Gangai have their own languages. Similarly, the whole spectrum of the caste-based hierarchy is to be found amongst the Hindu Madhesis. Brahmins and Kshatriya groups are situated at the top, while the Dalits at the bottom are considered impure and untouchables. There is also a substantial presence of the 'middle castes', like the Yadavas, Suris, and Kurmis. Caste divisions govern social relations and play a significant role in forming political choices. Very often they also shape economic stratification. (Hari Prasad Bhattarai: Cultural Diversity. P. 160)

There are many definitions of Madheshi according to many scholars. I would like to quote one of them here:

> "Madhesis are defined as non-Pahadi people who, regardless of their place of birth or residence, speak a mother tongue that belongs to the plains. However, in contemporary discourse, the category does not encompass the lowland indigenous ethnic groups and the Muslims. Indigenous peoples like Tharus, Rajbanshis, Gangai, and Dhimals, and Muslims have claimed that they have their own independent identity that is different from that of the Madhesis. Some groups, particularly Tharus, Dhimals, and Gangais, claimed that they are the original inhabitants of the Tarai and that the Madhesis are later migrants. "

There are many castes and cultures in Terai -Madhesh.

According to one scholar;

> "The word Tarai is derived from Persian language which means humid or muggy land. The Tarai plains stretch the length of the Southern Border and are home to half the total population including many non- Madhesh (both indigenous ethnic groups and recent migrants from the hill.)" Prakash Upadhaya: Nepali Culture and Society: P. 280.

Terai is also called Madhesh now a days because Madheshi people do not face identity crisis. The interim constitution has also recognized it. The historical two Madheshi movements have also focused on it to a great extent. Consequently Madhesh has its own monograms and testimony. Nobody can deny its existence in the true sense of the term. One Madheshi scholar has identified Madhesh in the following lines. Madheshi scholar like C.K. Lal has asserted that the term' Madhesh' refers to the cultural space where Madheshis reside. He said he preferred the term 'Madhesh'to Terai Basi because the word Terai carries the connotation of internal colonization. (2005).

> "Madhesh refers to the terai region specific to Nepal, approximate 23 to 35 wide broad belt of alluvial and fertile land stretching from Mahakali river in the west to Mechi river in the east between Indian border in the south and Sivaliks/Chure range in the North. Etymologically, Madhesh has been claimed to be derived from word Madhyadesh(mid country) or Matsyadesh(fish country) whose capital is said to be in Biratnagar. With the evolution along time, along with its historic values and usages, the word Madhesh has acquired cultural aspects into it that today it represents a way of life and different aspects of life -styles of people living specifically in the region. Whether it is Madheshi- Haat or Madheshi-colour, whether it is Madheshi cuisines or Madheshi *'boli-byabahar'*, the word has integrated different cultural aspects into it, and thus stands with a cultural connotations."

Vivaswan Kumar: Madhesh or Terai and Tharus or Madheshis: New Frontiers of Etymopolitics in Nepal: March 4, 2007.

Madhesh literary means mid-century (Middle country). It is Madhyadesh in Hindi. Madhese and Madheshi are two different words. First is derogatory where as the second one is acceptable to the all Madheshi people. Madhesh is an offensive marker of humiliation of the Madheshi Citizens in terms of geography and their colour. Madhesh is immensely marginalized in the polity and governance of the nation. It is still politically under represented. It is stepmotherly behaved by the Nation. The language and culture of the Madheshi people is not equally treated by the ruler elites. There has been a long tradition of discrimination and exclusion. There is also huge psychological division between Madhesh and Mountain since a long time. This type of division is not healthy for the sound health of the nation. Madhesh is a bread basket of Nepal. It covers the 17% of the territory of the whole country. It is also home of more than 40% people. It is a major source of national revenue and also centre of economic activities. The progress of the nation depends upon the progress of Madhesh in the true sense of the term. It is very important to address the main problems of Madhesh and the Madheshi people. It is also very necessary to fulfill their aspirations for the long term stability of democratic process, sustainable peace and progress in Nepal. Upendra Yadav has positive view regarding Terai/Madhesh. I would like to quote him here:

> "The Madhesh is the most important region of the Nepal, geographically and culturally distinct from the hills. However, the Terai region or the Madhesh of Nepal, could attract comparatively little attention of foreign scholars because it is hot, dusty and malarious. Consequently, little interest was taken about the Terai's geographical, historical, economical or cultural characteristics, despite the fact that it comprises 21% Nepal's land area which inhabits more than 50% of Nepali population. This neglect is striking, because the Madhesh is the backbone of Nepal's economy, producing about 65% of the nations gross domestic product (GDP) yielding about 76% of the governments revenue, and 60% agricultural products of the country. "(Upendra Yadav 2005, P. 18-19.).

Cheah (2008) says, "Madhesh not only implies a physical composition of the space that stretches across the southern belt of Nepal, but also includes the cultural and lingual space that exists as a basis of identity amongst many people residing in the region. "Similarly, the pioneer researcher and scholar on Madhesh, Gaige(1975) defined Madheshi people as those who speak plains' languages as their mother tongue or first language, whether they were born or live in the plains or hills. Bhattachan (2008) says(cited in Yadav, 1997),

> "Madhesh is a historical, political and sociological concept that refers to a group or communities discriminated by the dominant groups where as Teraibasi refers to any caste or ethnic group, including the dominant caste or group. "

Gaige and Hachhethu(2007) also define Madhesh as a plain landscape from Siwalik Hill range and the term Madheshi broadly encompass people of non-hill origin; their cultural identity is specially associated with the Hindu castes (from the plains) of Maithili and Bhojpuri speaking populations.

The Madheshi community is composed of the traditional Hindu caste hierarchy such as Brahaman, Kshatriya, Baisya and Dalits, and indigenous peoples, other native tribes and Muslims.

Madhesh, one of the three ecological zones of Nepal, covers 23 percent of the total land area and is 800 kilometers with its width varying from 25 to 32 kms. The boundary of Madhesh starts from the foothills of the Siwalik or Churia range of the Himalayas in the north and extends up to the Indian border in the south. Out of the 75 districts in Nepal, 20 districts, namely Jhapa, Morang, Sunsari, Saptari, Siraha, Dhanusha, Mahottari, Sarlahi, Rautahat, Bara, Parsa, Chitwan, Nawalparasi, Rupandehi, Kapilvastu, Dang. Banke, Bardiya, Kailali and Kanchanpur have been known as Madhesh(Jha, 2011). The total population of Madhesh constitutes 49. 3 percent of the entire population of Nepal, making it the most densely populated region of the Nation. (C. B. C, 2O11).

The residents of Madhesh can be categorised into Madheshi and Pahadi or hill communities. Madheshi people have been living in Madhesh for centuries with their own distinct language and dialects, unique pattern of dreaming and traditions where as the hill people are of hill origin and they came to Madhesh during the course of migration. Their tradition, culture and rituals are different from those of the Madheshi communities. (The Landscape of Madhesh. P. 118.).

Dilli Ram Dahal's opinion is also quotable here:

By ethnic/caste groups, Tarai encompasses the diverse cultural groups ranging from the hill origin(the Hill origin caste groups, Adibasi/Janajati and Dalits) to the Tarai-origin peoples or Madhesi caste origin groups including Tarai Dalits, Adibasi/ Janjati groups and others. In brief, the Tarai today presents a distinct multi-cultural region or the' melting pot' in terms of settlement of various groups of people.

No systematic and scientific study has been made so far in this field. The detailed ethnographic studies of the Madhesh community are limited. According to sociologist Dilli Ram Dahal:

"There is little disaggregated socioeconomic data on various groups of people of Nepal even today. In brief, little is known about the people of the Tarai even today, particularly the 'Madheshi people, with reference to their origin, history, culture, socioeconomic conditions and the processes of inclusion/ exclusion among them. "(Dahal 2013).

One of the most neglected areas of social science research in Nepal is the Tarai, a strip of tropical flat land, occupying 20 districts, where 50. 15 percent of the total population of Nepal lives today (C. B. S. 2011).

So, there is an urgent need of anthropological and sociological study of these castes. Every caste has its glorious history of its origin but there is no proper study is done in this regard. Every caste has religious history of its origin.

Only two of the origin tales texts are available so far they are Chitragupta Katha and Shri Chanwar Puran. Others have oral tradition to tale their origin tales. Very recently Deepak Chaudhary has wriitten a small book about Dev caste of Terai Madhesh which is his M. A. dissertation. Ram Narayan Dev has also added a volume to the study of Dev caste. Thus Dev caste has attracted the attention of the research scholars.

Previous studies: First of all Dor Bahadur Bista has written a book People of Nepal' on the basis of his field study which has proved a mile stone in this regard. F. H. Gaige (1975) has raised the Madheshi's burning issues very seriously and scholarly manner. Thereafter Rishi keshavraj Regmi has also written a book named Essentials of sociology and Upendra Yadav's book named Conspiracy against Madhesh is very thought-provoking. J.P. Gupta 's some books in Nepali Vernacular are also worth reading. Makhan Jha (1971) in his book The Sacred Complex of Janakpur' has tried his level best to explore various aspects of Janakpur's religious complex. A British scholar Richard Burgahrt (1978) has also concentrated on the Maithili culture and civilisation. This is a part of his PhD dissertation. Meena Acharya (1981) in her research work 'The Maithil women of Sirisa has focussed on the social, cultural and economic conditions of the women folk of the Mithila region in details. This is the first and last work done about the lifestyle of Maithil women. Haribansh Jha (1993) has highlighted Madheshi's multiple problems in his book 'Tarai Community and National Integration in Nepal'.

Deepak Chaudhary has written a good book named Tarai/ Madhesh of Nepal in which he has dealt with many major castes of Tarai/Madhesh. This scribe has also written two books on Madhesh' Janakpur, the Sacred Jewel of Nepal' and' Murder of Madhesh'. Kalyan Bhakta Mathema is a writer of Madhesh Uprising and there is a latest book on Madhesh named' The Landscape of Madhesh' edited by Ruhi Tewari and Anirudh Prasad Sah. Besides, some books have been written in Nepali Language also on Madhesh and Madheshi movements. Two Madheshi movements have inspired and motivated some Madheshi writers to write and think about Madheshi sentiments and sensibilities. Now they write in Hindi, Maithili, Bhojpuri, Awadhi and Bajjika in ever genre of their literature vigoriously but they are getting no incentives from the Nepal government. Recently the Culture Ministry of Nepal has started Vidyapati Kosh (treasury) to inspire and encourage the Maithili writers. It has also awarded some eminent writers for their outstanding works. This ia a good start and it will be appreciated by every one.

But it matters little that Terai/Madheshi scholars and thinkers have contributed substancially to the production of knowledge or that they have expressed their finest sensibilities in creative arts, architecture, poetry and literature. It is a matter of great regret that they have not been evaluated properly and intellectually. They have been behaved step motherly in each and every field of life. They are considered as second class writers and thinkers. In Republic Nepal the politicization of community identities draws historical traditions and perceptions. My own writings unfold the enchanting ethnic divercity of Madheshi communities and the variety in their social and cultural traits and engage with identity and representional issues and their relevance to the rise of Madheshi nationalism.

> "Caste prejudice in India is still very strong and ingrained and changes for the better can only be effected slowly. These castes form the majority of India's landless labour and they will have to be provided with land if their economic status is to be improved. "The same and similar condition is prevailing in Nepal also

especially in Terai/ Madhesh. (Religion and Communities of India: P. 122).

Now I am giving a short list of the castes of Tarai/ Madhesh.

Amat (Risley 1891) has described them as a cultivating caste of old Bihar. They profess Hinduism. Their tutelary deity is Thakurani, who is worshipped by their own priest. They also worship the god Mahadev. Festivals like Sankranti, Chaite Sankranti, Rathjatra and Rajaparab are celebrated. The astrologer (jyotish) helps them finalise dates for auspicious functions. They have oral traditions of folksongs and tales. They sing at Kirtans. P. 45.

The large numbers of Amats are found in eastern Nepal, from Jhapa to Parsa districts. The largest numbers of Amats are found in Saptari, Siraha, Dhanusha and Sunsari districts. Even among them, Saptari includes the largest number. They have been living in Tarahi, Barharpur, Fulkahi, Jamuna, kochebakhari, Sakhada, Lalapatti, Bhagawatpur, Partaha, Hanuman Nagar and Barsain of Saptari and in Inaruwa of Sunsari. The Amatts claim they are Kashyap by clan. (Deepak Chaudhary, 2011, P. 82).

Their total population according to the census of 2011 is 1,929 male and 3,830 female.

Agrahari

This community is mainly a business community which resides densely in the district of Sunsari. Their main concentration is in Duhabi, the eastern part of Nepal. They are also found in the districts of Rautahat, Bara and Parsa. They are expert in business. They claim that they are the descents of Agrasen, the emperor of Agroha (Haryana state of India). Their similarity is with Agrawals. The Agrawal community claims that Agrasen Maharaj (emperor) is their ancestor. They also claim that they are from Ayodhya, the Capital of king Dashrath. Their tutelary Gods are Sokha, Mahabir, Kali, and Narsingh. Their surnames are Gupta, Agrahari, and Sah. Their gotra is Kashyap but they are in Minority.

Deepak Chaudhary writes about Agrahari in the following lines:

> "The Agraharis also consider themselves as the children of Agrasen. In some places, marriages have been conducted between Agrawal and Agrahari. The Agraharis of Nepal identify themselves as the inhabitants of Ayodhya. "(Deepak Chaudhary:Tarai/Madhesh of Nepal:2011. P. 88-89.)

Badais

They are mainly carpenters who make wooden ploughs for cultivation. They also make bullocks carts for carrying men and materials from one village to another. They make tables, chairs, wooden cots and other furniture used by individuals and families. They sell their products in the village markets and earn money for their livelihood. (R. D. Rakesh. P. 37)

Deepak Chaudhary writes about Badais in his book Tarai/ Madhesh of Nepal in the following lines:

> "The traditional occupation of the Badais is related with wood, which means from Baradhika, a Sanskrit word, which means to cut the roots of Baradh tree. They specially worship Bishwakarma. In the west, the Badais are engaged in farming. The Badais use the title of Sharma. In comparision to the Lohars of the west, the Badais are more prosperous. Nowadays, the Lohars too have been doing the work of wood and the Badais also have been doing the work of iron. In this sense, they are considered intimate. " Deepak chaudhary, 2011, P. 94.

Baniya Trader/ Merchant

Baniya is mainly a business class caste. It has been divided into many groups such as Kathbaniya, Rauniyar, Kamlapuri . It has been originated from the Sanskrit word Banik which means vyapar (Business). It is also divided into many gotras such as the Kashyap, Bhardwas and Aliman etc. It has many surnames like Gupta, Rauniyar, Sah etc.

> "While caste endogamy is still maintained, it is now not as rigid as it was in the past. Marriages are arranged through negotiation. Though polygamy is permissible, monogamy is followed. Divorce is secured either through mutual consent or from the statutory law

courts. Widow and widower remarriage is permitted. Both nuclear and joint settlements are found. The rule of residence is patrilocal. Parental property is equally inheritated by all the sons. "

Baniya caste is generally vegetarian. Rice is their favourite food. Hinduism is their religion. The settlements of this caste are concentrated in the districts of Jhapa, Morang. Sunsari, Saptari, Udaypur. Siraha, Sarlahi, Mahottari, Dhanusha, Rautahat, Banke, Bardiya, Kailali, Kanchanpur, Makawanpur, and Nawalparasi etc.

Deepak Chaudhary writes about Baniya in the following lines:

> "The Baniya is the peculiar Madheshi word which means business man. It is believed that the Baniya comes from Banika, a Sanskrit word. The Baniyas are suppling the goods of daily needs. There are different sub-groups in the group of Baniyas too. The Baniyas have medium type of socio-economic position. The sub-groups of Das/ Kathbaniya and Kamalapuri exist in very small number. " (Deepak Chaudhary 2001, P. 84.) There is a very popular proverb regarding Baniya 'Raja rijhabe ta kanver sun, Baniya rijhabe ta Chhatak bhar nun. It can be translated like this if you please the king then you will get sufficient gold and if you please Baniya then you will get one Chhatak of salt only. There is also one saying 'Baniya Baikal' which means Baniya people are like beggars."

One scholar has written about this caste in the following lines:

> "The Bania caste in the village is internally quite a differentiated one constituting some sub-castes, most notably the Kalwar and Teli. However, all of them believe that they are the direct descendents of Lord Shiva. They maintain that their style of life has always been ascetic and sattavic(truthful) characterised by vegetarianism. Therefore, they claim that they are more pure than, or as pure as, anyother caste including the Brahmins. They argue that, apart from creating and earning wealth, they have also, successfully performed the role of Kshatriya, a notable example being the establishment of the Gupta empire. " (Ed. Dipankar Gupta: Gaurang R. Sahay. P. 119.)

Bantar (Craftman)

The main occupation of this caste is to weave baskets using bamboo. The very word means Bans which is bamboo. This is their traditional craft in which they excel others. Their other occupation is fishing. They are skilled labour in thatching of houses made of bamboos and straws.

According to some sociologists Bantar has been identified as:

> "It is plausible that this community name is derived from the word 'Bans' meaning bamboo in Madhesh. The Bantars are a composite of four subcastes, namely the Majhi, the Hazra, the Bate and the Panza. These sub castes are divided into a number of lineages. "(K. S. Singh, 1994 p. 141)

Deepak chaudhary has mentioned in his book Tarai/ Madhesh of Nepal about Bantar in the following lines:

> "The facial features of the Bantar come to the scene as mixed, resembling even Tharus. In some places, they have also established marital relationship with the Tharus. There are many similarities between the Tharus and the Bantars of Morang and Sunsari districts. In Morang and Sunsari, some Bantars are great landlords too. "Deepak Chaudhari: Tarai/Madhesh 2011 p. 137).

> According to one finding'They are heavily concentrated in the Eastern Terai region. Bantar population, of more than 1000, are found in 5 districts. Morang has the highest Bantar population followed by Saptari and Sunsari. '(NNDSWO. 2006. P. 26.)

Now they have become very conscious politically. They do not want to hide their identity as Bantar. They have been indentified and enlisted under Dalits (downtrodden). They are indeginous nationalities of this region. They speak Maithili in the east and Bhojpuri in the middle region.

According to one linguistic survey 'Maithili was the major language spoken by this community in the study area. Hindi was considered as their second language. For writing purposes they used Devnagari script. Some of them were also found to speak Nepali language. (NNDSWO. 2006. P. 27.

They reside in Jhapa, Morang and Kapilvastu districts of Nepal but their dense population is in Morang, Sunsari and Saptari districts. Their settlement is also found in the Gangetic plain. They reside in the joint family. Some of them like to live in separate family because they are up-to-date now. They use the surname of Sardar. They have also some other surname such as Dahit, Raut, Mahato, Bachhar and Singh. Rich families use ornaments made of gold and silver. Women of this community put on parda (veil) to cover their face.

According to one finding:

> Some three hundred years back, Bantars were heavily concentrated in Pipara village of Bara district. They were attacked by a Muslim headed by Iliyas. This led them to flee from there to different parts of Nepal. Those who remained in the village were compelled to raise pigs and as a result, Iliyas stopped attacking them. They are found in Morang, Saptari, Sunsari, Mahottary and Sirha in large number. They have their own informal council to settle disputes and take major decision on community affairs. They claim to have relatively higher social status than people belonging to Dom, Musahar, Halkhor, and Mehtar communities. According to the population of 2011 their total population is 82, 191.
>
> The population of Bantar caste jumped from 35,839 to 82,191 in the census of 2011. This is a happy news for them.There is a very interesting story about them. King Bhimsen once happened to visit the place called Rajghat(Sunsari district). The king was thirsty and to quench his thirst he requested some water from the Bantar brothers. The younger brother feared and hid inside his home, locking the door. The elder brother, without any fear, provided water to the king. Because of this incident the younger brother was called Dhokewal and the elder Raj Bantar. (NNDSWO, 2006, P. 27-28)

They have different clan Names such as Sardar or Sirdar, Majhi, Dhokewal, Dhodh Banatar, Das Rajbantar, Pajaha and Jaanth. Most of them use Sardar because it is their clan name.

Barais (Paan sellers)

They sell Paans to the customers as well as Grihasta meaning landlord. This is their profession from generation to generation. Chewing Paan every day is the habit of some aristrocat people. It is a luxurious habit. They are occupational castes. They have a prominent role to play on the auspicious occasion of marriage. They serve Paan to invited guests on the auspicious occasions. Deepak Chaudhary writes about this caste as follows:

> The group of Barais traditionally engaged in selling betel nut is found in each of the districts in mid-tarai and in Nawalparasi-Banke. They do not have enough land though many of them are working as farmers. They earn their living by working as labourers in the field, i. e. hiring(in local language say Adhiya/ Batiya) other's land for farming and taking of the production. They are backward in educational, social and economic aspects. (Deepak Chaudhary: 2011, P. 97)

They are famous for making tasteful Paans. They can prepare Paans according to the tastes of their clients as well as customers in no time. They also serve Paans to the visiting guests on several occasions of marriage, Mundan, sacred thread and other family gatherings. Now-a-days they have their own betel shops in villages, bazzars and towns. They make money by selling Paan with sweet spices as well as Zarda(tobacco). Pan with Zarda is considered cancerous for mouth. (R. D. Rakesh, 2005, P. 36.

Barber

The barber is a general aide in all feasts of most of the castes of Tarai-Madhesh. He is supposed to bring water for most of the castes on several occasions such as marriage ceremony, Satyanarayan Bhagwan Puja, sacred thread ceremony and also on the occasion of death rituals. His main duty is to shave the hairs of heads of the people.

Barnwal

This caste is limited to the region of Mithila. They are found in numbers in Saptari, Siraha and Sunsari. Their ancient history is also available according to which Ahiwarn was the 21 emperor of Manghat of Ayodhya. He established a town which name was Barn. It is believed that they were Suryabanshi because they are descents of the same dynasty. According to the story mentioned in the Mahalakshmi the king Parmal and Ahiwarn were contemporary. They also established their kingdoms in that time. It is the general belief of people that they have their origin from that dynasty. Barn city is also related to Buland city. In 1912 the Mugals attacked on India. They also captured Burn city. Thus this caste is also found in Bihar of North India. They use the surnames of Lal, Barnwal, Gupta, Prasad, Anand, Kumar Chaudhary and Singh. They are now professors and lawyers. Some of them are in the Government service. They are very practical caste of Nepal.

Deepak Chaudhary writes about Barnawal in the following lines:

> "Most of them do Bratabandh. They have nearly 36 Gotras. The Varnawals, engaged in farming, extend from the eastern Nepal to Dhangadhi in the west though in small number. The socio-economic situation of the Varnawals is not satisfactory. " (Deepak Chaudhary: Tarai/Madhesh of Nepal:2010. P. 91.)

Bhedihars

They are occupational castes who are supposed to be owners of sheeps. They are also called Gaderiya. They can be distinctly recognized in the community becase they rear sheeps and goats. There is one family in the village of Sisautia in Sarlahi District. They are called as Bhedihar and use the title of Pal such as Bhikhari Pal. He is from Rautahat district and resides in Baneshwar and does business of vegetable spices. He has also a grinding machine. Most of them are farmers and tame sheeps and goats. They also take them for gazing in the fields of village. They also trade in hairs of sheeps which they cut time and again. They are densely populated in Sarlahi, Rautahat and Rupandehi. They are not highly educated. So they are not serviceholders. Their education is limited to intermediate to bachelor. Some of them are in service now-a-days but not holding higher posts. Generally they are not in good economic condition. Deepak Chaudhary writes about this caste in the following lines:

> They used to rear sheep and sell Kebada (a kind of useful grain given to sheep and goats;it is found in the forest and is costly too.) Deepak Chaudhary 2011, P. 98.

Brahmin

Brahmin caste has also been ruler because it belongs to the ruling elite. In the words of Meghnad Desai:

> "The beauty of Hindu society is that the elite rule by dividing people into a thousand cells, telling each that it is higher or lower than the other. This is how the Brahmins ruled for centuries without a powerful State to give them sanction. "(The Repulica daily 3rd Sept. 2012)

Brahmins are the highest ranking caste in the Hindu hierarchy. They have also political dominance to some extent. They are big landowners and highly educated. Brahmin falls into two groups. Maithil and Mahapatra. Maithil subcastes are comparatively more rich land owners, moneylenders and educated. They hold high posts in Government jobs and in private sectors also. Mahapatra Brahmins conduct death rituals during the funeral ceremony. They also act in Shradha karm as priests. They are given gifts on the auspicious occasions of Satyanarayan pooja and marriage ceremony. The Brahmins were the most privileged in the contemporary social hierarchy (R.K. Chaudhary, 1976).

According to one scholar:

> "King Harisimha Deva introduced Kulinism by which the Maithil Brahmanas were divided into four subclasses:Srotriya, Yogya, Panjbadh and Jaibar, and the Kayasthas. The latter was further divided into two, Kulina and Grahastha. Around the time the system of Panjiprabandh came into use according to which a collection of the genealogical data of each individual was maintained and these Panjis were collected and consolidated by 1313. It is said that the system was introduced to protect the 'purity of blood' by making people record their ancestry which help in avoiding the forbidden degrees of relationship in contracting marriage." (Religions and Communitics. P. 64 65.)

But now a days Kayastha is a separate caste quite different from Brahmin.

The total population of male Brahmin terai is 69,468 and female number is 64,638.

The great saint-poet of India has this view about Brahmin which is much more appropiate in the context of today:

> "The brahmin who flies into a rage at the touch of a mahar,

-That's no brahmin

The only absolution for such a brahmin
Is to die for his own sin.
He who refuses to touch a Chandal
Has a polluted mind.
Says Tuka, a man is only as chaste as his own belief.
Tukaram.
(says Tuka. trans. Dilip Chitre, New Delhi, Penguin Books, 1991.)

Beldar

Beldar is also known as Loniya. It has historical origin from the time of Sher shah. The word Beldar is derived from the *word bel'* meaning a digging implement and dar refers to the person who handles it. The Beldars use a bell for digging earth. This caste is engaged in construction and road measurement from the very beginning.

Crooke (1896) mentions that 'Beldar is a general term for the aggregate of low Hindu tribes who make their living by earth work.

Bhumihars

They are also land owners, moneylenders and traders and claim themselves as superior as Brahmins but they are inferior in social status to them. They do not perform as priests rather Maithil Brahmins serve as their priests for domestic rites and rituals. But now-a-days they are also placed in good jobs private and public both. They are also very active in politics. (R.D. Rakesh 2005. P. 35) There were many big personalities in the politics of Nepal as well as India such as Ram Narayan Mishra and Bhadrakali Mishra. S.N. Mishra was the foreign Minister of India. Birendra Mishra was one of the members of Election Commission. Now they are holding higher positions in each and every walk of life. There is only one family of Bhumihars located in Pipara V.D.C. of Mahottary district which is famous in whole Nepal.

Deepak Chaudhary has written about Bhumihars in the following lines:

"It is believed that Bhumihar is the corrupted form of the word Bhumibal. It is said that the person who ploughs the earth using the plough is called Bhumihal(Bhumihar). In Tarai, they have earned their fame as well-known landlords. The educated and elderly people say that Bhumi(land) and Har/Haar(garland) make the word Bhumihar, the meaning of which turns out to be'producing crops from land'. They are more influencial especially in Mahottari and Sarlahi districts in Nepal. The largest numbers of Bhumihars live in Mahottary, Sarlahi and Dhanusha districts. (Deepak Chaudhary. 2011, P. 66.

In census of 2011 Bhumihars have not been registerd as a separate caste. This is a matter of great regret in the opinion of sociologists. Not a single caste should be forgotten in the census of a country. This is a big mistake. So Bhumihars are not happy because they have been accepted as a separate caste in Tarai/ Madhesh society. They have high position in the caste hierarchy and wear holy thread like Brahmins. They consider themselves equal to Brahmins in the caste hierarchy. They also use the titles of Jha and Pandey like Brahmins.

There are different sub groups in Bhumihars caste of Madhesh. They are known as Dighwait Bhumihars because they came from Dighawa, those who came from Eksar of Baliya as Eksariya and those who came from Jhansi as Jhijhautiya Bhumihars. The Mauwar group has not been considered as a superior one.

Some other sociologists have different views. Bhumihars are described as the ethnic group emerging from the Kshatriya father and Brahmin mother (Shastri, 2002. P. 30).

Some of the Bhil (tribal group of RAJASTHAN, India) claim themselves as Rajput. 'Intermingle of Bhil and Rajput is called Bhilala and Bhumihar' (Lal, 1991, p. 87)

At the time of Dharmapal Sen (A. D. 1420-1433), Bhumiyar Brahmin Prithvi Singh had been on the rule of Gorakhpur and Champaran of North India (Khanal. B. S. 2061).

According to one scholar:

"The Bhumihars claim that, though they have been performing the Kshatriya role in society, they belong to the Brahmin Varna. They

> believe that they are traditionally a powerful landowning Brahmin caste that had long back stopped performing the roles of a Purohit(priest). They claim descent from those Brahmins who performed the consecration rituals for Ajat Shatru, who had achieved kingship by dishonouring and killing his father, Bimbasar. In return, king Ajat Shatru donated large landholdings to the Brahmins. Other Brahmins oppossed this act, and socially differenciated themselves from the former. That is why, the Bhumihars argue, they do not have marriage relationships with the Brahmins. However, they claim that they belong to the Brahmin varna, and are as pure as other Brahmins and purer than other castes." (Gaurang R. Sahay. P. 118.)

Chamar or Raidas

Risley (1891) writes that according to the Puranas, the Chamars descended from the union of a boatman and a chandal woman. But scholars identify them with the Karewara or leather worker mentioned in the 10th chapters of Manu's Dharmashastra. The father of the caste was a Nishadha (offspring of a Vaisya father and a Brahman mother). In U.P. and Bihar states of India they are also called Raidas. They are also called charmkar and Harijan. They are also called Mochi. A great poet of Nepali literature Banira Giri has composed a poem entitled Mochi. Their community name is derived from the Sanskrit word Chamar, meaning leather worker. The Chamar is one of the major communities found in almost all states of Northern India and as well as in other regions. (K.S. Singh. The Scheduled Castes. 2010. P. 304.)

> They are shoemakers. They make sandals, drums, soccerballs and bicycles seats out of leather. They carry the carcasses of dead animals out of the village. They are hired to play drums in the musical bands on several occasions. (R. D. Rakesh 2005. P. 38.)

One Indian scholar has written about this caste in the following lines. I would like to quote here:

> "They continue with their traditional craft of shoe-making but the new generation is taking to agricultural labour, industrial labour, business and government service. " (K. S. Singh: 2010, P. 322).

Most of the Chamar caste are the followers of Hinduism. They worship Hindu Gods and Goddesses in their daily life.

They have their own tutelary Gods too. They worship Kali, Nandi, Goraiya, Lakeshowri, Raktamala, Meera (mugo), Kuhelini, Gahil, and Narsingh. These are some of the deities they worship with devotion and dedication. Supan Bhagat Ram is their ancestral deity which is very popular in this community.

They are divided into three subgroups, namely Goriya, Nahahia and Jaiswar. They all have the same Gotra Kashyap. They use surnames such as Ram, Das, Satnami, Rohit, Ravidas, Ramnami, Rishi, Ruidas, and Raut. They are mainly landless. They are now employed in leather factories as tanners and cobblers. They also make shoes and repair them and polish. Satnami chamars are religious minded but rest of them are traditionally disposer of dead bodies of animals. They are also supposed to eat the meat of animals except cows.

"Traditionally, it is believed that the Chamars helped dispose the dead body of animals as their occupation. At present, they make different domestic products from the animal hide. Besides farming, they have been also engaged to doing physical labour and mending bags, shoes and other things in the urban areas." (Deepak Chaudhay P. 134.)

Mythology: According to the mythology there were four brothers in a Brahmin family. They were not supposed to throw away the dead animal of their home because they were from upper caste. It was a big problem for them. So the youngest one threw the dead body of animal hanging his sacred thread on the branches of a tree. Consequently he was not allowed to enter his own house because of loosing the supremacy of his Brahmin caste. From that day his successor came to be known as Chamar.

There is another mythology regarding the origin of this caste. According to which Supan Bhagat Ram was endowed with supernatural power. Once upon a time Bhim one of the brothers of Pandavas who was supposed to have strength of thousands of elephants was asked to pick the rudraksha that was hung on the tree but he failed in his attempt. Supan smiled upon his failure and plucked it within no time. He was proud of his success and claimed that it was only possible because of his true devotion and dedication to God. He was true devotee of God. He declared that if you are true devotee of God then He bestows power irrespective of your caste.

> According to one study conducted by NNDSWO it has been revealed that Ravidas was believed to be a sincere devotee of Lord Ram. In the study area, Chamars with the surname 'Ravidas' worship Ravidas once a year. Kanduk Rishi, popularly known as Bantha Chamar, a wrestler by profession was also considered to be a devotee of Ram. Lord Ram was believed to be very happy with his devotion and sent him to heaven. In that period it was believed that people belonging to low castes do not have space in heaven. (NNDSWO, 2006, P. 36.)

Now they have changed their old profession. Traditionally they used to beat drums for informing the villagers on the occasion of big festivals and eclipses. They were also supposed to preinform them about any necessary gatherings. They used to beat the Dhol (a kind of musical instrument) in the whole village for any necessary information for which they were supposed to get some remuneration. They also used to play Rasanchouki on the auspicious occasions of marriage ceremony. Besides it, they used to play pipahi, dhol, narsinha, mridang, nagara, tasa, khurdak and so on and soforth. Now they play on Angrejibaja (English band and concert). Some members of the Chamar community of Sarlahi have come to Kathmandu and joined the modern concert and Band groups and play on the auspicious occasions of marriage ceremony. They are same and similar caste of Kathmandu valley's Sarki caste. The women of Chamar caste are supposed to be expert in delivery cases and some times in abortion cases also. But now a days they are not supposed to take such cases in their hands because they are not medically safe. Before that when nurse service was not available in the remote areas and also in rural areas they used to work like nurses. Sometimes it proved very fatal.

In terms of population size, the Chamar is the largest Dalit community among the Madheshi Dalits. Chamars with more than 10,000 people, are found in 12 districts of Madhesh. About Dalit there is a poetic expression, I would like to quote:

"How long must we endure this terrible tyranny?
Must we live like prisoners of war until we die
My soul had roared out Zindabad.
Innumerable suns lit with blood
Go now from city to city, setting them on fire.
(Dhasal , Raktani Pette le Aganita Surya.)

This caste is very old one. I would like to quote here to support my statement:

'Members of the Chamar caste claim that they belong to the Chanwar Vansh (lineage) which had ruled over a large kingdom for many years. The first king of this lineage was Chamundarai, descended from the sun, the god of light. Thus, those who belong to this lineage are, in fact, Suryavanshi. The Chamars believe that they lost their kingdom and came to occupy a lower position in society because the last king of this lineage committed a blunder by disobeying the lineage norms and rules. They regained their earlier Kashatriya status only with the emergence of saint Raidas- the reincarnation of the Sun— as a member of their caste. He further states:

'The Chamars claim that since they belong to a Kshatriya lineage and have originated from the Sun, they are as pure as any other caste. The Chamars cite the Shri Chanwar Puran, a religious text, to substantiate their belief. Members of the Chamar caste believe in the authencity of this text, which they read out during their caste ceremonies and ritual performances. The local Brahmins, on the other hand, vehemently deny its religious authenticity and authority. ' (Gaurang R. Sahay. P. 117).

Chidimar

Chidimar refers to the group of Nomads. They live on hunting birds. They are also called Kadoriya in the local language. They wander hither and thither and hunt several birds. They usually live in tents and camps. They have no permanent houses to line in . Their financial condition is not good. Nowadays they work as labourers. They always keep moving with their family. They can eat any thing they get. They can eat cats and dogs which they kill. They are known as Sikarijara and Satara or Savara which means those who kill birds. Most of them are non-vegetarians. Their main food is rice and wheat. Men and women of this community mostly drink alchoholic drinks. It has been mentioned in the Schedule Castes of India about this caste in the following lines:

> "The Chidimar are divided into different exogamous lineages called bansa, whose main functions are to indicate ancestry and regulate marriage alliances. The vermillion marks on the forehead, glass and lac bangles, and veiling the head and face from certain kin and outsiders are the signs of a married woman. (K. S. Singh 2010 P. 361)"

Deepak Chaudhary writes in the following lines about Chidimar:

> "Chidimar refers to the group that earns the livelihood by hunting birds. In Madhesh, they are also called Kadoriya. They are wanderers. Though hunting birds is their main occupation, now- a-days most of them have been working as labourers. They follow Hindu tradition regarding festivals and rituals. "(Deepak Chaudhary 2011, P. 145). "

In India they are included as a scheduled caste under the nomenclature of Chandhai Maru. It has been mentioned in the scheduled castes of India. I would like to quote here:

> "The attitude towards education is not very encouraging. Monogamy is the rule, but sororal and no sororal poligamy are also encountered. The vermillion mark on the forehead, glasses and the bangles, and veiling the head and face from certain kin and outsiders are the signs of a married woman. "(K. S. Singh 2010, P. 361)

Hunting is their traditional occupation. Rope making is very popular in this community. There is an easy access of this community in local and village market in which they sell their products.

Danuwars

They are the largest of the three groups (Majhi, Darai) under discussion and are scattered throughout the low hills of eastern Nepal and in theTerai in addition to these found in Kathmandu Valley. Very few are found in the areas west of Kathmandu Valley. They are found in the northern part of Mahottary district seem to have followed the pattern of Tharu social organization. Their village councils settle disputs. (Dor Bahadur Bista: People of Nepal: P. 142).

They are very simple people. Their settlement is scattered in Tarai and Hill area. So they have mixed life style. I have found one Danuwar family in V.D.C. Brahmpuri of Sarlahi district. All the members of this family are like general Madheshi. They have fair complexion and use sacred thread.

Danuwars are of three types. Those living along the upper river valleys are called Kachhare (living in Kachhar). Those who live in Tarai/Madhesh are termed as Rajhans. Third type is also known as Bahaduria. Rajhans are considered superior. I would like to quote:

> "A few of the Danuwar family names that exist in that are kumar, Singh. Rae and Khan. They are the same names found among several other ethnic groups of Nepal, but are nothing more or less than family names in this context. " (Dor Bahadur Bista, People of Nepal 7th edition. P. 142)

Danuwars living close by other peoples, including Tharu consider themselves the highest caste. They claim that they belong to royal family because Giri Narayan Puraditya established a small state in the areas of Saptari and Siraha districts. Kuleshwar Singh Danuwar was also the king of the Pakariyagarh state. Durgarai Danuwar was the famous wrestler of that time. He was also royal wrestler of king Kuleshwar Singh. He had hundreds of disciples, among them Salhesh was the first and formost. So they regard themselves as the descents of the Karnat dynasty.

"The people of the plain area of Teenpatan, Chitwan were called Droniwar or Dronawar during the medieval period, and at present it has become Danuwar' (Nepal, 1998, P. 288).

Nathuni Singh Danuwar, former M. P. and writer, writes in his book'Indigenous Danuwars' in the following lines:

> "While the Hindus were moving away through the way of the Sindhughati, the Danuwars began to rule over 'Doran Dihi, from there they were called Donawar/ Danuwar. His opinion is this that the Karnatak Dev king of Simraungarh, was Danuwar. It is believed

> that the last king of Tirhut, Harisingh Dev, after Muslim attack, ran away near by the river Kamala. He was followed by so many men and women including some Danuwars. He died on the way in Teenpatan in Sindhuli district. It is said that since then Danuwars are residing in Sindhuli, Ramechhap and Sindhupalchowk districts. Even at present, the Danuwars consider themselves as Rajputs and Karnat kings as their glorious ancestors."

Danuwars are the indigenous people who are like Majhi and Darai. They have their own separate identity. Most of them live in the Terai belt. They also live in inner valleys. So they do not have the same mother tongue but their culture resembles with the Tharu people. (Ram Dayal Rakesh, 2005, P. 39).

Anthropologist D. B. Bista writes in his book named People of Nepal:

> "In their appearance, attitudes and behaviour, they are not different from Tharus. They are dark, and seemingly body, yet display great health and strength. Like the Tharus, they are considered to have developed immunity against malaria. ' (D. B. Bista: 2007. P. 128).

According to the census of 2011 their total population is 84,115.

Some scholars have thrown light on the historical background of Danuwars. I would like to quote here:

> "In the 14th century, King Bhupal singh, the sixth generation of the Karnataki dynasty established by Nanyadev, ruled over the Kingdom of Simraongadh. Initially he was the vassal of Nepalaeuwar, but later gained independence under the guidance of his chief minister (kulmantri) Chandeshwar Thakur. This was followed by the invasion of the Muslim king Gyas-ud-din Tuglak, which came in full swing and could not be resisted by Bhupal Singh, so he had to flee with his wealth and some subjects northwards along the banks of the Bagmati river. "(Rajesh Gautam/ Asoke K. Thapa. Magar: 1994. P. 141).

There are three types of Danuwar namely the Rajan, Tharu and Rai. The Rajan Danuwar are considered the highest on the Danuwar Thar heirarchy, so much so that some even wear the sacred thread or Janai, like do the Brahmins. They use

Brahmin priests to perform rituals from birth till death. (Rajesh Gautam 1994). They have Kashyap gotra like other Hindu castes. They worship their Kul Devata with respect and reverence. Tharu Danwars are second on the heirarchy rank. The Rai Danwar are the third and last or lowest in the Danuwar Thar heirarchy. Their society is very similar to that of the Kiranti. Their settlements are found in Makwanpur and Udaipur in hilly districts and in Sapatari, Siraha, Dhanusha, Mahottary. Rautahat, Bara, Parsa. Sunsari and Morang districts of Terai, Madhesh.

They use to speak Hindi, Maithili, Bhojpuri, Awadhi and Nepali but they now use their own language as their mother tongue. They have their own written literature. Nowadays they do not use their own script though some people say that they have it. Now they have adopted Deonagri script. The Gorkhapatra Daily has provided special provision for some national languages in Deonagari script, Danuwari language is one of them.

Danuwars are the indigenous people who are like Majhi and Darai. They have their own separate identity. Most of them live in the Terai belt. They also live in inner valleys. So they do not have the same mother tongue but their culture resembles with the Tharu people (R. D. Rakesh 2005, P. 39.).

> "In their appearance, attitudes and behavior, they are not different from Tharus. They are dark, and seemingly bony, yet display great health and strength. Like the Tharus, they are considered to have developed immunity against malaria. " Dor Bahadur Bist:People of Nepal: P. 128.
>
> The settlements of the Danuwars exist from eastern Nepal and even in the districts of Himalayan region. They are the oldest inhabitants of the hot weather of Madhesh. They speak Maithili and Bhojpuri languages which they call as Danuwar language. They follow the Hindu tradition and culture and their lifestyle and complexion resemble to that of other Madheshi groups (Deepak Chaudhary. 2011. P. 194.)

But now they have developed their own language and there is literature also. The Gorkha patra also publishes literary articles twice in a month. So their language has been recognized as a separate language.

> 'The people of the plain area of Teenpatan, Chitwan were called Droniwar or Dronawar during the medieval period, and at present it has become Danuwar' (Nepal, 1998, P. 288.)

Some Danuwars reside in the hilly region also. They have some different customs from those who live in the plains. One scholar has this opinion about Danuwar:

> "In the beginning of winter, the Pahari call upon the Danuwar from Makawanpur District to perform a special ritual aimed at protecting their livestock against disease and wild beasts. This rite is called Pherilaune in Pahari and Nepali. Danuwar men conduct the rituals in the forest. They are paid in cereal by all village households. The total population of Danuwar is 84,115 according to the census of 2011. Gerad Toffin:Newar Society: City, village and Periphery: P. 276.

Dev

Two scholars have done comendable job in the anthropological study of Dev caste of Terai/ Madhesh. They are from the Dev community. One is Deepak Chaudhary and other one is Ram Narayan Deo. Their books are worth reading in the field of Anthropology. Deepak Chaudhary's book Nepalko Dev Samuday and Ram Narayan Dev's book entitled Maithil Dev Jatik Itihas aa Sanskriti both are wrtten in a nice manner. Deepak Chaudhary has written his book in Nepali Vernacular where as Ram Narayan Dev has wriiten his book in Maithili which is the second language of Nepal. Their approach is research oriented. Both the books are authentic because the scholars are native. So, it is believed that they have very honestly contributed to their community. Now-a days this theory has been forwarded in the field of anthropology that scholars should themselves write about their own caste and community. This will be much more convincing and reliable and readable. Deepak Chaudhary has written about Dev in the following lines:

> "The number of Devs, living especially in Saptari, is very small. Nothing is mentioned about the Devs in Maithil caste system. One belief is that with the end of the Karnat dynasty, they escaped

> towards the north-eastern part and reached upto Saptari. In Saptari, there is Sakarpura V.D.C. where the Devs have large land ownership. It is also heard that Sakarapura was named after Shankra; Shakra Singh Dev (possibly Shankar Singh Dev)." (Deepak Chaudhary: Nepalko Dev Samuday: P. 49.)

Their settlement is centered mainly in one village named Sakarpura which falls in the district of Saptari. They claim themselves that they belong to Karnat dynasty and they have their favourite Goddess named Shakhda Chhinmasta Bhagawati. It is also believed that king Shakra Singh had established Shakarpura village, surrounded with canal. A famous historian has also supported this view in the following lines:

> In this way, though any reliable source is not available, certain facts like statue of Bhagwan goddess established by Shakra Singh, Shakarpur village(possibly its name was Shakrapur in the beginning) and the remains of Lalpatti, justify that Shakra Singh, the king of Simraungarh, had established the temple of Shakhada Goddess (Harikanta Lal Das, 1999). They also belong to Vaishya Varna. Their marriage custom is similar to Maithil Brahmin. First of all they follow the principle (Sidhant) and confirm marriage ceremony after consulting the geanology of the bride and bridegroom. Panji tradiion is very popular in the Dev community like the Maithil Brahmin. Panji is the chronological record of gotras prevelent in this community from the very beginning. This system was started by Hari Singh Dev in 1127. The person who keeps this record is called Panjikar. It also proves that this caste is very ancient. They are very much educated and occupy prestigious post in publc and private service. There is cent percent literacy among them.

They celebrate Madhushrawani festival with great pomp and show every year in which married girls take part. This festival is celebrated by the Maithil Brahmin, Sonar and Dev castes.

There was no mention found about this caste in the census of 2001 but according to the census of 2011 their total number is 2,147.

Dhanuk

Crooke (1896) notes that the Dhanuk are a low tribe who work as waterman, musicians at weddings and their women as midwives.

Russell and Hiralal (1916) noted that they were a low caste of agriculturists whose origin, as given in the Padma Purana, quoted by Sir Henry Elliot opined that owing to their occupation of cultivation, the Dhanuks enjoyed a comparatively better social position. Etymologically, the word Dhanuk is said to be derived from the Sanskrit word dhanuksha which means archer (Rose) Deepak Chaudhary writes about Dhanuk in the following lines:

> "The settlement of the Dhanuks extends from Jhapa to Parsa districts. Their education and socio-economic situation is not satisfactory though. In the western Tarai, it can be seen that some Dhanuks of the east are working as rickshawpullers and labourers. In course of the author's study, the Dhanuks were not found with their permanent settlement in the west of Parsa district. The Dhanuks are mostly found using the surname of Mandal. Their facial appearance resembles the mixture of castes. " (Deepak Chaudhary 2011, P. 80.)

In the words of Mukti Mandal, a Dhanuk Expert and writer of Dhanuk Darpan has cited a mythology:

> "The people entitled with Dhanuk are the children of Dhanak MUNI of the ancient Videh state. Dhanak Muni was the king of the state of Videh during Satyayug (in Hindu mythology, there are four ages or Yugs :Satyayug, Dwaparyug, Tretayug and Kaliyug; Satyayug was the first age.) King Janak of Videh also belonged to the same dynasty. He was given a bow by Lord Mahadev. During Sita's marriage, the very bow was kept for the Swayambar(a function in which the bride chooses the groom). Lord Rama broke the bow. King Dhanak had four sons and Kritabirya was the eldest of them. Later on , he was defeated by Parshuram. Due to the fear of the loss of the Dhanuk dynasty and for their own protection, they lived under pseudonym and gotra began to live in the region as general being. So they feel proud of being the descent of his dynasty. They have four branches such as Siroha, Dudhawar, Magahiya and Sura. There is matrimonial relationship among them. They consider only gotra to decide marriage arrangement.

The name of their family deity is Andhi Mandal. They also worship Gahil, Goraiya, Dharamaraj, Bishahara, Kali and Meera. They have their own caste system i. e. Chaurasi and Sabha (assembly). Chaurasi is considered as respectable caste because it solves all problems arise in the community. They have Brahmin priests for performing all rites and rituals from birth to death.

I have written about Dhanuks in my book entitled 'Janakpur: The Sacred Jewel of Nepal :

> "They are another large agricultural castes in the Mithila region. They have vote-banks in their hands. Originally they are good archers. They are also called 'clean castes'. Now-a-days they are much more educated and engaged in politics, business and social activities. Some of them hold high posts both in private and public sectors. There are three types of Dhanuks such as Mandal Dhanuks, Suri Dhanuks, and Rajbanshi Dhanuks. (R.D. Rakesh, 2005 P. 36.)"

Doms

They are basketmakers. They make baskets and Dhakis from the bamboos and sell them in the village market. They also make several useful articles from the bamboos according to the demand of the villagers. They also rear bears (pigs) for their livelihood. They act as assistants on funeral rites. They have very important role to play at the time of funeral rights because without their help this rite can not be solemnized properly and purely. They are given gifts of food, cash, clothes on the occasions of solar and lunar eclipses. (R. D. Rakesh P. 38).

They place themselves in the Sudra Varna. Traditionally they are acrobats. They are well known for their rope dance and acrobatics. Musical instruments are used. They excel in the craft of basketry. Agricltural wage and mat-weaving are other sources of income. The Dom accept water and cooked food from all communities. They also participate in the village car festival.

> They profess Hinduism and worship the Hindu gods and goddesses. They also worship their Istdevtas, Patmisri and Moulis at the family level. Mongala and pura are the village deities. (K. S. Singh, 2011. P. 473).

Doms are considered to be one of the lowest untouchable caste groups of Madhesh. Their total population, according to the 2001 census, is 8931. The Dom population with over 100 are found in 12 Terai districts. Their scant population is found in every district of Madhesh because they are occupational caste. They are very useful castes in terms of making Baskets, Tokaries, Dalia, Maur (Made for bride grooms to wear on the occasion of marriage). Their handmade things are used in daily house hold works. They are fond of pigs. They graze them in dirty places in the vicinity of their villages.

Myth: There is a mythology about Doms which says that once Mahadev, God of Gods and his consort Parvati invited all tribes and castes of the world to a Mahabhoj (fabulous feast). Therefore father named Supan Bhagat reached late. So he was bound to eat left over. Since then Doms are called eaters of leftovers.

There was practice among Doms some five or six years back that they themselves used to go to collect left overs of any big feast, thrown by big men in the villages of Terai-Madhesh. But now this practice is dying out day by day. They are considered untouchable in the Hindu society.

They have lost many of their traditional customs and cultures and are seen to have gone through a drastic metamorphosis. In India, there are Ankuriya Dom, Bisdeliya Dom, Wajniya Dom, and Madhiya Dom. In Nepal, Maidhiha Dom live mostly in eastern and central region where they have thars (sects) like Chirniya, Ledwar, Wirjiys, Bhakraith, Pokhariya, Jonhjha, Ludhier etc. (Gautam and Magar 1993:185).

There has been a study conducted by Nepal National Depressed Social Welfare Organisation which states, I like to quote here:

> "In the study area, when some one from another caste dies, there was a tradition of buying a pyre from a Dom. In exchange, that Dom is given cash or sometimes even cow or buffallo. Hence it still believed that "mare pachee dumai raja" (a Dom becomes a king when some one dies). It was also learnt that Doms do not allow people belonging to other communities to touch them on Sundays. If accidently some one touches them, they purify themselves by taking a bath. (Ethnographic Study of Terai Dalits in Nepal. 2006. P. 52)

Doms are mostly Hindus and they worship all Hindu Gods and Goddesses but they were not allowed to enter the Hindu temples generally. Now they have been categorised as Dalit and now they have their identity. They are not considered as untouchables. Now a days they use surnames such as Marik. Bechan Marik is a famous astrologer and gemologist. He lives in the vicinity of the famous temple of Pashupatinath in Kathmandu but he is originally from Dharan.

National Dalit Strategy Report, 2002 states that any other caste member of the Terai except Halkhor does not accept water and cooked food from Doms. If any member of the high caste Hindu group is ever touched accidentally by them, he/she must purify either by sprinkling 'gold water' or taking bath in the pond. But now a days they donot have such social stigma to suffer. They are still suffering from the caste-based discrimination any how or other. I would like to quote here to support my statement.

> "Among the other dalit groups in the study area, it was found that Doms are worst hit by the caste-based discrimination. They were not allowed to share the common resources like drinking water. They accept food and water from other communities but hardly any communities accepted from them." (Ethnographic Study of Terai Dalits in Nepal. 2006, P. 57.

Literacy rate among the Dom community is very low. Their children do not go to the village schools regularly. So drop out percentage is very high. Some of them have completed primary standard but most of them are illiterate. Their main profession is basket making from bamboo. Their settlement is scattered from Mechi to Mahakali. They make bamboo products such as baskets, fans, and nanglos, mukut, especially made on the occasion of marriage for bride. Actually they are bamboo crafters by profession since time immemorial. They also prepare harhara and farhara made of different colours on the same occasion for this purpose. They sell it in local market on the occasion of several festivals especially during Chhatha festival in which it is needed most. In the earlier days they were not supposed to take money directly from the buyers but they put money on the ground and only then they used to pick it from the ground. But nowadays change has occurred in their daily life. They can take it directly from the buyers. Now they used to live in urban areas. They are very useful caste by profession. They used to light fire for the person cremating the dead in exchange of some cash or kind. The Dalit Commission has categorised them as Dhanikars which they do not like because they (Dhanikars) think themselves superior to them. Dhanikars do not eat left over. They also carry lights and lamps to lead the marriage party to different places of pilgrimage especially to the place of local deity for seeking blessing.

Origin: Older people believe that they are in existence from the Ramayan period. When Rama came to Janakpur with marriage procession to marry Sita, he saw many leaf-plates outside one house. He thought that this must be the same house where there was marriage feast. They could easily findout that this was the house of Dom who used to eat left over on any ceremony such as Satyanarayan Pooja and marriage ceremony. King Janak became unhappy to know it. So he issued an order for them not to make more than one-storey houses. They live in cluster at the end of the village. Their houses are made of mud, having straw roofs. They do not own their own land. Pig trading is the main source of their income. There is pig farming big or small in each family. It does not cost much more money because pigs graze in open latrine in village. This scene looks very dirty.

Dhanikars and Doms are like two brothers. Dhanikars are richer than Doms.

According to the population of 2011 their total population is 6, 668.

Dhobis

Dhobis are also occupational caste whose main work is to wash clothes. The very word Dho means to wash in Hindi. This is their traditional occupation. They are considered as untouchables and are denied access to various public places like so many sacred places of prayers such as temples. They are also not allowed in hotels and restaurants. However, the discrimination they encounter is relatively less offending than that of other Dalit groups.

"In addition to their traditional occupation of washing clothes they are also employed in government and private services. They speak Hindi and use the Devnagari script for all kinds of communication. They profess Hinduism and worship Gods and Goddesses of the wider pantheon. Brahmins are their sacred specialists who are called upon to perform marriage and death rites. Though monogamy is the norm, polygamy is permitted. Vermillion, lac and glass bangles, bindi and toe-rings are the marriage symbols for women. "(K.S. Singh 2010. P. 448).

They profess Hinduism in their daily life and worship Hindu Gods and Goddesses. They are very useful caste in the community because they wash clothes of daily use very nicely. I would like to quote:

> "They are Hindu by religion. Their principal deity is Ghatoia or Ghatmata the landing place of Lord Shiva or pond where they wash clothes. They also worship Ashapura Devi and Bheraji. Their sacred specialist is (Panditji) is a Brahman. Holi, Rakshabandhan, Dussehra and Diwali are some of their important festivals. The Dhobi of Bihar suffix surnames like Ram. Baitha and Prasad. (K. S. Singh:2010, P. 449.) In Nepal Dhobis use surname of Rajak.

Their presence is considered auspicious on the occasion of marriage ceremony. On the auspicious occasion of sacred ceremony (Jagyopapit or Janeu or Bratbandh) their presence is considered pious because it is necessary that Dhoties should be coloured by them. At the time of travelling outside of homes it is good to see them. It makes travelling husslefree.

I would like to quote here:

> "Nowadays, they are attracted to education also. We can find a number of these people with a high school degree. Their family deities include Kalibandis, Mahamaya, Sokha, Dharmaraj, Karik and Bishahara. They use the surnames of Rajak, Saphi and Chaudhary. (Deepak Chaudhary: 2010. P. 137.)

Due to urbanisation they are attracted towards towns and cities. They have started opening laundry in city areas because they are having brisk business. Now they face acute problem in the city areas because of want of sufficient water supply. Water bodies are drying up day by day. They have started home delivery system in the urban areas where as they go to door to door to collect dirty clothes in the village areas. They also go to door to door to give washed clothes. They get annual remuneration in cash and kind. In this way their standard of living is going up. Now they are educated and engaged in government service.

There is a mythology related to this caste which says that Lord Krishna once went to Dhobi place, where his maternal uncle Kansha's clothes were given for washing purpose. His intention was to put on his clothes to disguise himself as Kansha for entering the palace to kill Kansha but he did not get success in it. This mythology is quite enough to prove that this caste is very ancient. The great epic Ramayan also proves that this caste was in that period. There is a saying that one man from the Dhobi community blamed Rama for accepting Sita after her abduction by Ravana without any verification. Dhobis are of two kinds such as Dhobi and Rajdhobi. According to one study:

> "There are two groups in this community viz. Dhobi and Rajdhob. Dhobis still continue with their traditional occupation. In contrast, Raj dhob who used to wash clothes of kings and wealthy people in ancient times have left their occupation and were seen engaged in various other occupation and like farming and rickshaw pulling. Dhobis who were found to be engaged as agricultural labourers cultivated land on share crop basis (Bataiyya system in their own language). (NNDSWO 2006. P. 48).

This caste is very useful. So every village of Tarai-Madhesh has this caste. This caste goes to waterbodies for cleaning clothes. It is a matter of great regret that it cleans the dirty clothes of all villagers but treated as untouchable. According to one study it has been clear. I would like to quote:

> "They were considered as untouchables and are denied access to various public places like temples and restaurants in the study area. However, the discrimination they encountered was relatively

less than that of other dalit groups. It might be due to their relatively sound financial status." (NNDSWO 2006 P. 49.)

Washerman and barber are necessary for auspicious ceremonies. It is understood that theses castes were created according to the demands of royal court as well as small rulers and landed proprietors. I would like to quote here to support my statement:

> "The functions of the washerman and barber necessary to purificatory ceremonies have struck him, and he seems to regard the corresponding castes as having been created by local imitation of royal courts on a small scale by petty rulers and landed proprietors, each of whom must have, like the divine or royal model, a barber and a washerman and other ritual functionaries, sothat there grew up classes of people each performing separate ritual functions, which classes developed into closed castes." (J. H. Hutton:1963. P. 176-167).

> "Rajbhars believe that they belong to the Khastriya varna because they constitute a sub-caste of the Rajput. They claim that they too are Raghuvanshis belonging to the lineage of king Raghu. They argue that the difference between them and other Rajputs is not a caste difference but a class one." (Gaurang R. Sahay: Caste in question P. 118.)

They are mainly washermen. They wash clothes on daily wages or according to monthly or annually contract. They do not wash only but press the clothes which make people smart when they wear it. Now they have laundary in the village markets and towns. People are fond of them. (R.D. Rakesh P. 37.)

"In addition to their traditional occupation of washing clothes they are also employed in government and private services. They speak Hindi and use the Devnagari script for all kinds of communication. They profess Hinduism and worship Gods and Goddesses of the wider Pantheon. Brahmans are their sacred specialists who are called upon to perform marriage and death rites. Though monogamy is the norm, polygamy is permitted, Vermilion, lac and glass bangles, bindi and toe-rings are the marriage symbols for women." (K. S. Singh. 2010. P. 448)

Thus it is clear that Dhobis are Hindu by religion. Their favourite gods are Ghatoia or Ghatmata. They are worshippers of Ashapura Devi and Bheraji. Their family priest is a Brahmin who performs their all rites and rituals. They celebrate Holi, Rakshabandhan, Dasain and Diwali. The Dhobis of Nepal Terai suffix surnames like Ram, Baitha and Rajak.

Deepak Chaudhary has written about Dhobi in his book in the following lines:

> "Traditionally, the work of Dhobis is to wash clothes. In the marriage of a girl, their presence is essential. Similarly, at the time of Bratabandha, as people believe, the clothes should be coloured by Dhobis. In some places, during the marriages and death ritual of this group. Brahmins are also invited but they do not take food. Due to a growing urbanisation, the Dhobis are thriving with their occupation. " (Deepak Chaudhary: Tarai/Madhesh 2011 P. 137).

The total population of Dhobi is 109,079 according to the census of 2011.

Dusadhs

They are economically very important castes because they are sturdy and stout in physique and are good labourers. They serve as Chaukidars (village police) in the village at night. They are employed by the village community to keep vigil in the village at night. So, they act as watchmen. They are also called Paswan. They are becoming politically conscious day by day. (R. D. Rakesh 2005. P. 37).

A study done by Nepal National Depressed Social Welfare Organization also supports that they work as Chowkidar. I would like to quote here:

> 'Dusadhs in the study area also claimed to do the work as Chowkidar or watchman. Many young adults males have migrated to different parts of India like Delhi and Punjab to engage themselves in various types of jobs. A number of Dushad men were also blamed as dacoits in the past. " (NNDWO, 2006. P. 62)

They still suffer from caste-based discrimination in the rural areas of Terai-Madhesh. They are not allowed to share the waterbodies situated in their vicinity with other caste/

ethnic groups. They accept cooked food and water from other communities but it is a matter of great regret that no community accepts food and water from them.

Some people believe that Dusadh is the corrupted form of Dusadhya, a Sanskrit word, referring to being extremely. Others also believe that Dusadh is one of the succeeding generation of 'Dushasan' of the Mahabharat. Traditionally, they were the guards of landlords. Though farming is their main occupation, most of the Dusadhs have been doing the work of physical labour. They are living in each of the districts of Madhesh. Their surnames include Paswan, Dusadh, Das, Ram and Hajara. (Deepak Chaudhary 2011, p. 136).

But it is wrong to say that Dusadh's surname is Ram.

> "They are non-vegetarians, but abstain from taking pork and beef. Rice is their staple food. They take alcoholic drinks and rice beer which are either available in the market or made at home. They smoke beedis, and chew tobacco, khaini and betel leaf. "(K. S. Singh 2010. P. 505.)

Salhesh is the patron God of the Dusadh (Paswan) caste of Terai Madhesh. It is worshipped by this caste every year on the auspicious occasion of New year. A big fair takes place on this occasion at Mahisautha, Salhesh Foolbari (garden) and Patari Pokhari (pond) and also in the premises of Salhesh temple. This lush green garden falls in the Siraha district four kilometers far from Lahan near by the East-West Highway. There is a Haram Tree near by the temple of Salhesh. In the middle of the Haram tree blooms and appears a garland of flower. It is of white colour. It is a wonderful sight which attracts visitors from India and Nepal. It is said that beloved Dauna could not get the love of Salhesh throughout her life. So she appears once in a year like a garden of flowers and enjoys the imaginary company of Salhesh and fades away the next day. It is still mysterious. No body knows this secret till today.

Historian and famous scholar of Maithili culture Radha Krishna Chaudhary writes about Salhes-Puja in his book 'Mithila in the age of Vidyapati:'

"Salhes has been worshipped since time immemorial as a hero in the whole Mithilanchal. According to some historians he belongs to the 16th century. He was the Chaukidar(watchman) of king Kuleshwar Singh Danuwar. There is no controvercy in local legends. According to legends and researchers this fact has been confirmed. After the death of King Giri Narayan Puraditya Singh King Kuleshwar Singh established the Pakariya kingdom. There is a mound in the Pakariya Garh. That mound is in V. D. C. of Amahi of Siraha district. Durgarai Danuwar was a famous wrestler of that time. He was the royal wrestler of King Kuleshwar Singh. All facilities were provided to him by the state. He had hundreds of discilples, among them Salhes was the first and foremost. There was a big stadium in the kingdom. There was a good arrangement of stadium. Salhes defeated all the wrestlers of that time. So he became hero of his time."

"Once in a year the dance is performed at the Salhesa-sthan where Dusadha and other castes of the village assemble together with flowers, and other objects of worship. Decorations are simple but quite representative of the occasion. The priest utters mantras and after sometime begins trembling showing thereby that king Salhesh had entered his body. Thereupon he shouts, runs and moves on the edge of the sword. He then goes on throwing flowers and uttering blessings on those who offer various presents to please the God. After sometime the priest comes back to his normal form and the celebration is over." (Radha Krishna Chaudhary: P. 389).

Gonds

According to Crooke (1974) Gond probably means inhabitant of Gauda or western Kosala. Gond is synonymous with Gonr. They are non-vegetarians who take pork, and their staple food wheat, Jowar and Maize are supplemented with local millets like Sama, Kodo, Mero and Mijri. Both men and women consume alchoholic drinks. They smoke beedis and cigarettes and chew tobacco with betel leaf. (K. S. Singh: 2010. P. 562.)

There are seven subgroups among them. They are Dev, Gond, Dholi, Kolam, Kaila, Bhut, Mudipal, Padol and Raj Gond. According to a study conducted by a team of scholars (including this scribe alongwith Deo Narayan Dadav and Hari Sahani in the district of Rautahat) found their settlement in a village near by Garuda Bazar. No study has been made in Nepal about this caste but in India some scholars have done some study. I would like to quote:

> "The rule of residence is patrilocal. Either of the spouses can divorce and remarry. Nuclear and ventically extended families are common. Male primogeniture is the rule of inheritance and the eldest son gets some extra land and utensils. Succession is followed from father to son and the eldest son gets the fathers' authority. (K.S. Singh; 2010. P. 503.)

Gwalas

Gwalas prefer to be called Yadavas now a days. They are in the majority in all the districts of Tarai/Madhes. They play a pivotal role in the politics of Nepal as well as in Bihar and U.P. states of neighbouring country India. They are now highly qualified and employed in all sectors whether private or public. The present president belongs to Yadava caste. He is the first president of the republic of Nepal .

According to sociologist Dilli Ram Dahal 'they are numerically the highest in the following five districts of the Tarai: Siraha and Saptari (Eastern Tarai) and Dhanusha, Mahottari and Sarlahi (Central Tarai). Yadavs are popularly known as Ahir, Gwala or Gwar (milkman) or simply Yadav. In the social stratification of various Hindu groups of the Tarai which is a highly stratified society. Yadavs place themselves in the middle of Hindu caste group (Dahal 2005, Bista 1967, Gaige 1975).

> "They include the Abhiras or Ahirs of Northern India, Raos of Haryana, Gwallas of Uttar Pradesh, Mandals of Bihar, Pradhans of Orissa, Ghoshala of Bengal, Gopas and Reddis of Andhra Pradesh and wadeyars of Karnataka. " (Religions and Communities of India P. 138)

Some historians think that the Jats are Yadavas in origin, that the Gujars and the Marathas were also Yadavas and that they and the Gujars intermarry. The princely houses of Baroda, Bikaner and Alwar chose to align themselves with the Rajputs, though their roots were in Yadava stock.

After the defeat of many Yadava dynasties and principalities of the south, the Yadava peasantry was overpowered by high-caste Hindus. The tending of cows, their principal occupation, which was once held in high esteem, began to be looked down upon.

The Yadavas claim themselves Chandravanshi Kshatriyas. They are very dynamic in their daily life. They are classified in the scheduled castes category in India and in Nepal they are classified in O.B.C. but they nowadays claim themselves as an indigenious Nationalities. Socially, economically and culturally they are superior than many castes. They have very robust personality. They are very strong to look at. According to one Indian scholar:

> "The Yadava contribution to the composite culture of India is immense: the nomadic art forms, the Abhira language (Apabhramsa), the Raslila and certain ragas like Ahir-Bhairav, Abhirika, Gopixa, Kannadaguala, and perhaps most of all, the Krishna cult." (Religions and Communities of India. P. 138)

One Indian scholar has written about Yadavas in the following lines:

> "The Gwalas are the great pastoral caste of India. Their main occupation is the keeping of cattle and the sale of milk and dairy products though most of them have land as well as. Socially the Gwalas rank with Kurmis and others from whom the Brahmanas take water. Then there are the Kumhars, Lohars, Barahis, Hajamas, Mellahas and so on. Next come the Beldars, Naunias, Tantis and Teli. These last rank very low, so much so, that the mere sight of them is deemed by some people to bode ill and only degraded. Brahmanas perform their ceremonies. Equal in rank are the Kalwars, or distillers of liquors. Tha Pasi tap palm and date trees, a few make mats and even hunt and sell game. Lower still is the washerman. " R. R. Diwakar: Bihar Through the Ages. P. 695.

Yadavas were called Ahirs also long time back. They are the major castes of Hindu caste group. They claim themselves that they are the descent of Indo-Aryan Kshatriya dynasty. They consider themselves as the children of Yadu. So they belong to Yadu dynasty. Yadu was the Kshatriya king of mythological period. According to the Hindu mythology, the Yadavas were the children of Yadu. So they call themselves Yadubanshi. Lord Krishna was Yadubanshi. Now a days Yadavas also claim that Krishna is their favourite God. He was very fond of cows and cow-herds. He used to rear cattles in the forest of Brindavan.

It has been mentioned in the Gopal Rajbanshawali:

> "First of all, the Gwala dynasty (dynasty of cowboys) also called Gopalvanshi dynasty which ruled over Nepal. During the regime of the Gopal dynasty, eight kings ruled here and the first of them was Bhumi Gupta. The Gopal dynasty was succeeded by the Mahishpal dynasty. Its three kings ruled Nepal in the course of time. After that the Kirats who belong to the eastern Nepal came and attacked and defeated the Mahishpals. They became the rulers here.' (Kirkpatrick, 2007) has written about Mahishpal dynasty in the following lines:

> "The Mahishpal regime began with the kings of the Rajput Gwalas. They used to live in Tarai that was situated between Simraungarh and Janakpur, and had their armed forces also. They came to Nepal when they got the news that Yaksha Gupta of the Gopal dynasty was childless."

It has been mentioned that the Yadu dynasty ruled over the Kathmandu valley three thousand years ago. (Chemjong 2003) is of this opinion:

"The first Kirat king who ruled central Nepal was Banasur. His kingdom was conquered by a king whose name was Bhuktaman of the Gopal dynasty. The Kirat folklore mentions that when Krishna came to know about the establishment of the Kirat rule in Central Nepal, he sent a strong force of the Yadav tribe under the command of Bhuktaman to conquer the kingdom of Banasur. Bhuktman attacked Banasur, killed him and established his new kingdom. Thus the kings of this Yadav dynasty ruled over central Nepal for eight generations."

Deepak Chaudhary writes about Yadavas in his book Tarai/ Madhesh of Nepal in the following lines:

> "The people who came from the Nanda dynasty have been found using the title of Raya. In Nepal, they are also called Majharaut and their main settlement is found in the mid-tarai regions. The people who came from the dynasty of Gwala are known as belonging to the Gopal dynasty in Nepal. The Gopalis of Kathmandu come under this group. Farming and rearing cows used to be common occupations to them in the past. In Tarai, the Gopalis are called Gwala. " (Deepak Chaudhary:Tarai/ Madhesh of Nepal. P. 76-77.)

Their settlement is found from east to west and north also. They are in majority from the view point of population. In north they are called Gopalis who reside in Palung, Thankot, Balambu and Tistung and according to latest research they have very similar occupation. Again I would like to quote Deepak chaudhary to support my statement:

> 'We can find the settlement of the Gopalis in present Thankot, Balambu, Tistung and in the places like palung. The Gopal dynasty and the Mahishpal Dynasty used to adopt their own occupation. Those who reared cows belonged to the Gopal dynasty and those who reared buffaloes belonged to the Mahishpal dynasty. '(Deepak Chaudhary 2010. P. 75)

Gwalas or Yadavas are strict followers of Hinduism. It has been mentioned in the Hindu scriptures. The Mahabharat is the true testimony in which the Yadavas have been described as big warriers. Lord Krishna alongwith Arjun had leading roles in the great war. Lord Krishna belonged to the Yadava dynasty. So it is crystal clear that this is very ancient caste group.

As mentioned earlier that they are Hindus, so they worship Hindu Gods and Goddesses. They have unflinching faith in village deities like Gahil, Kali, Dharamaraj, Bishahari, Jalpa devi etc. Their favourite God is Rajaji whom they worship as Gramdevta (village deity). I would like to quote here:

> "The Yadavas orYaduvanshis believe that they are true Kshatriyas because their forefather is Yadu, while the Rajputs or Raghuvanshis claim descent from his brother, Raghu. Both Raghuvanshis and Yaduvanshis believe that they belong to the lineage of Manu. The Yadavas concede that they have been occupying a lower politico-economic position than Rajputs for a long time. The reason was

> that Yadu, their forefather, had disobeyed the unjustified demands of his father who, in the capacity of the king of a large kingdom, disinherited him and did not allow him to act as a prince. Nonetheless, the Yadavas argue that since they belong to the lineage of Manu, they are not at all impure or less pure than any other caste. " (Gaurang R. Sahay. P. 117-118.)

They use the surnames of Goit, Gurmaita, Marwaita, Kusiyat, Biraji, Sethwar, Isanaut, Bisnaut, Deshwar, Bharkhet, Adhikari, Ray, Gope, Chaudhary and so many but Yadava is very popular because of dominant politics of this caste. They have many subgroups within them such as Manjharaut, Krisnanaut, Sethbar, and Bisnaut, Bharkehr (Raya, Goit, Marbita, Gurmaita, Kusiyar and Biraji, Raut Choudhary 2008. They have also very strong ethnic organization in all the Terai districts. They were elected in the majority during the C. A. election. They hold high posts in the academic fields, in the beaurocracy and in the private sectors also. In the 1999 General Elections, out of 42 Madheshi Members of Parliament in the 20 districts of the Tarai, 11 Members of Parliament(26. 2%) were Yadavs. Similarly in the Constituent Assembly Election 2008, of the total 601 MPs, 199 MPs were were from the Madheshi groups and of them 46 were Yadavs(23.1 percent from the Madheshi groups (Election Commission 2008). They celebrate various folk festivals such as Dasain (Dashahara), Durga pooja, Diwali, Chhath and Holi with pomp and show. Marriage rituals are performed at the bride's house. They marry within their caste groups and inter-caste marriage is rare among them". In other words, considering the caste structure and hierarchy among the Tarai Hindu caste groups, inter-caste marriage is still not encouraged among Yadavs and all other groups. Like the other Hindu Madheshi caste groups of the Eastern and Central Tarai, they perform and celebrate all Hindu rituals and festivals". (Dahal 2013) The dead bodies are cremated and a mourning period of thirteen days is observed. The Shradha ceremony is celebrated on the twelfth day.

According to one scholar Yadavas have been Aryanized long time back. I would like to quote here:

"The propensity of the Yadavas toward Sanskritization is evident from their attempt at Aryanizing their history. The first history of the Yadavas was written by Kithal Krishna Khadekar, and published in 1959 under the title The Divine Heritage of the Yadavas. The book situated the origins of the Yadavas in the Abhirras and than the ruling dynasties mentioned as Yadavs in the Mahabharat and the puranas. Most of these caste histories try to demonstrate the Abhiras were of Aryan origin and that Rewari is the last representative of the Abhira kingdoms." (Christophe Jaffredot: Religion, Caste & Politics in India: P. 455.).

The Yadavas claim that they are Aryans in order to enhance their status within caste society. Thus the Yadavas largely because of the influence of the Arya Samaj, remained imbued with the ethos of Sanskritization. I would like to quote here:

"In appearance, they proclaim their Aryan descent. They are tall and wiry, have dark eyes, long noses, black hair and their complexion varies from wheatish to dark brown. Though mostly agriculturists, they also make good soldiers. The British enlisted them in their army though they had fought against them in 1857. They had a proud record as soldiers in the First and Second World Wars; a few even received military honours during British rule. In the annals of Indian military history there is sufficient proof of Ahir bravery that is immortalised in the ballads of Alah and Udal of Bundelkhand. " (Religion And Communities of India: P. 140).

According to one recent study it has been found that Yadavas have been categorised in O.B.C. but they have been put separate because they are more advanced and urbanised and educated than other castes which have been categorised as O.B.C.

I would like to quote here:

"While Yadavas technically fall within the O.B.C. category, they have been kept as a separate category because they are a relatively less deprived layer. " (The Landscape of Madhesh. 2012. P. 12).

One Nepali scholar has written about Yadavs in the following lines:

"The Yadavs are perceived as a middle caste in Nepal's Terai. Like all other castes, there are substantial class differentials among them.

But many Yadavs have ownership of some land. They are sizeable in number across districts, especially in eastern and central Terai. And they have become increasingly influential politically. I would like to quote here the most suitable saying about Yadavs:

> "Yadavs of Tarai are taking the lead in terms of occupying key political and administrative positions in Nepal as a whole. They are the most actively participating political group among the Madheshi groups in Nepal. So, simply labelling the Madheshi people as excluded without understanding their social, economic and political situations of people is the myopic way of dealing with and using the term, social inclusion. In other words, Yadavs are not at all excluded community in the given economic and political indicators of the society. But at the same time, there is systematic exclusion of gender and lower caste groups by Yadavs in their everyday lives. So, the concept of social inclusion and exclusion is not a single package to deal with as the same group differs in the given social economic and political indicators of the society (Oommen 2009). "

Their main occupation is agriculture. They raise domestic animals like cattle, buffaloes, cows and goats. They used to sell milk and curd from door to door on barter system. They also used to sell it in the local market but now a days they use to sell to the local dairy. They are comparatively and relatively rich in terms of land holding. I would like to quote here:

> "In medieval times the Ahirs gave up their arms and took to agriculture. In early British settlement reports they are spoken of highly as farmers. "

According to the census of 2011 the total population of Yadav is 1,054,458.

Hajaam/ the Barbers

Hajams are very useful caste of Tarai- Madhesh. They are needed on many auspicious occasions such as birth anniversary, marriage and death. They are also considered very clever caste in the sense that they are very practical. There is a very popular saying in the Madheshi community' Jatma Nauya and kagma kauya' which means a barber is very clever in the caste like crow in the bird community. They serve as messenger in the Madheshi society. They are supposed to go even far villages to inform people about marriage and other auspicious occasions for their presence on such occasions. This is very important work done by them. No body can do this work except them in the community. Their main duty is to shave hair on such occasions like Bratbandh (sacred thread ceremony), Bibah (marriage) and death. They also help Brahmins on such occasions. They not only shave hair but also trim it in a beautiful manner. They have aesthetic sense too much. Their women are also lovers of beauty. They cut short nails of women of the community.

There is also a legend related to its origin. Bidhata (Creator of this universe) created a man from his Navi (naval). As he was created out of the navel, he was named as Nai. Barber is also called Nai in the local language. So he was thrusted the work of trimming and shaving hair. They are involved in all Hindu rites and rituals from birth to death along with Brahmins. So they profess Hinduism in their daily life. They worship all Hindu Gods and Goddesses but their favourite god is Vishwakarma. There are many sub-groups in this caste such as Kanaujiya, Awadhiya, Tirhutiya and Byahut. Most of them have Kashyap gotra. They are very popular and useful caste in the Tarai/Madhesh community. All castes take water from this caste. This is also customary for them to receive guests with fresh water. They are also supposed to fill pitchers with fresh water and saplings of mango plants on the many auspicious occasions. This custom is considered sacred in all castes. This is also customary for them to perform on all auspicious occasions.

According to the census of 2011 their total population is 117,758.

Halkhor

The very word Halkhor symbolizes the utmost dirty works. This caste has deep rooted caste origin, based on Hindu system. They are said to be migrated from Bihar, India during drought time. Halkhor is a Maithili word on the basis of work of particular group of people, this word has been coined. Ancestral work of this caste was and is to sweep roads, to clean dirty places inside hospitals and toilet. This caste's ancestral profession was and to some extent is begging for food items and cash for livelihood. There is an equal word Mehtar who used to clean bath rooms. It is an occupational caste. This caste is very useful for the Madheshi society. This caste has its origin in the Hindu system. Their concentration is mainly in urban areas such as Janakpur, Birganj, Rajbiraj and Nepalganj. In these city areas they can get jobs very easily. K. S. Singh writes about this caste in the following words: " The term Mehtar, meaning a prince or leader, is an ironic title given to the people who are traditionally engaged as sweepers and scavengers and are known by different names in different parts of the country. They are also called Bhangi. Scavenging is their traditional occupation.

Halwai

This caste is also called Kanu. But there is slight difference betrween the two. Kanu is supposed to prepare soft food stuffs like Bhuja and Murhi. This is light food good for day time tiffin. This caste was engaged in making such type of food stuff in rural areas of Tarai-Madhesh. They fry beaten rice and rice in earthen pot under fire. This is a local method of making fresh refreshment taken after lunch. They do not take cash payment for this but some portion of beaten rice and rice. They also fry maize and chana for this purpose which is very popular easy eatables. It is also digestive and healthy for health. Even patients also enjoy it. It is dry and there is no oil in it.

Halwai people make different types of sweets and sell it in local market. This is a roaring business nowadays in rural area as well as urban area. Halwai people are also hired for big parties like marriage, Tilak, sacred thread ceremony. They are expert in making different types of sweets according to the taste of their customers. Formerly they used Pure Ghee in it but nowadays they use Dalda and Purified Oil. Now we find several sweets shops both in rural areas and urban areas. They also cater according to the order of their customers and make money. Most of them are vegetarians. Deepak Chaudhary has very candidly differenciated between the two in the following lines:

> "The Kanus and the Halwais are the same caste groups. Both of them are engaged in the business of sweets. It is said that the separation occurred later on, for some people, the Halwais separated from the Kanus and for others the Kanus separated from the Halwais. Traditionally the occupation of the Kanus is the business of different kinds of soft food (Murhi/ Bhujia) make made from rice and the Halwais are engaged in making sweets. But now besides their traditional occupation, they are also working as farmers, labourers and holding other jobs. Both of these groups can be taken as two sides of the coin. " (Deepak Chaudhary: Tarai/ Madhesh of Nepal: P. 89.)

Their local deity is called Lord Govind whom they worship every year with respect and reverence. His son is Ganinath whom they worship equally and respectfully. Lord Ganinath is their family deity. Praful Kumar Singh Maun has written a book highlighting his life and personality. They worship him in the month of Bhadra (August/September) every year regularly. Their Gotra is Kashyap. They use surnames such as Gupta and Sah generally but Rajeshwar Nepali is a veteran journalist and writer of this caste who do not use either Sah and Gupta. Likewise Radhe Shyam Lekali also does not use his original surnames. He is also a noted writer of Nepali language and literature. Yodha Shah of this caste was the secretary of The Nepal Government. Radhe Shyam Lekali is currently president of NRN Literary Association.

According to the census of 2011 their total population is 83,869.

Jogi

Jogi means a wanderer caste. It is usually referred to as Nath or Kanphata Jogi, they claim decent from Baba Gorakhnath. Jogi is the corrupt form of Yogi and they are considered to be followers of the Yoga system of philosophy founded by Patanjali (Russell and Hiralal, 1916). They are considered expert in yoga practices.

Many of them lead an ascetic life and sing songs in praise of Raja Bhartari. As regards dress, the ascetic branch of the yogi can be distinguished by their large earrings, saffron robes and sarangi (a single string musical instrument) (K.S. Singh, 2010 P.)

Deepak Chaudhary writes in his book Tarai/Madhesh of Nepal about Jogi in the following lines:

> "The Sanyasis or Yogis are taken as the children of the hermits of the mythological period. The liberal meaning of the word is to be involved in meditation being away from the social and family life. They are also called Yogis. The Sanyasis living in Tarai are enjoying the culture of Tarai. There is the tradition of putting Nath at the end of the name for the temple of Lord Mahadev; Pashupatinath for example is one. "(Deepak Chaudhary: P. 71-72).

But he has put Yogi/Sanyasi/ Jogia in one group. There is difference between Yogi and Jogi. He has highlighted Yogi in his above-mentioned book. He has not mentioned about Jogi. There is a long tradition of Sanyasi. They belong to Dashnami community.

Sanyasi tradition has been prevalent among Hindu of Indian subcontinent from very ancient times. It has its own identity. Mostly Hindu dominated Indian region and Nepal there is a lot of Sanyasi community. In the name of Dasnami tradition there is an organized community whose population is 6% of the total population of Nepal. It has been originated from the Sanskrit word Nyasi which means sacrifice. San is the prefix. So this complete word means the supreme sacrifice. According to Nepali Brihat Kosh (Nepali big dictionary), there are different meanings of Sanyasi. Such as one Ashram which is totally detached from this mundane world. Secondly one of the four last stages of Hindu tradition. Thirdly detached from the worldly pleasures and involvements, there is a separate religion-Yog Religion. Fourth to denounce every thing at sweet will.

According to Encyclopaedia Britannica:

Religious ascetic who has renounced the world by performing his or her own funeral and abandoning all claims to social or family standing are generally buried in a seated posture of Meditation(http/www. Britanica.com).

Sanyasis are of two kinds: original. Sanyasi and Grihastha Sanyasi. One who has renounced home and resides in Temple or in shrine and who has returned from temple or shrine and leads homely life. Those who have adopted Sanyasi tradition and those children who are born of this tradition are called Dasnami Sanyasi. Those who follow Shaivaism of Hinduism regard and respect First Jagad Guru Shankaracharya. He is supposed to be of eighth century and he was born in the Kalti village of today's Kerala state of South India (Sharma, 2039 B.S. 72). He has written the essence of the Upanishad, Bhagawat Geeta and Badrayan and supported the Adyaita principle on the basis of Badrayan's Brahmasutra.

Braham Satyam Jagan Mthya jivo Brahmaiva Napar.

Sanyasi tradition has been prevalent in every age. According to it Guru Sanyasi or Acharya has been in every age as follows:

Age– Acharya Sanyasi

Satyayug – Vishnu, Brahma, Shiva

Tretayug– Shakti, Parashwar, Vashistha

Dwaparyug– Vyas, Shuk, Shounkadi

Kaliyug– Gawdacharya, Balgovindacharya and Shankaracharya.

There are 23 Acharya Sanyasi according to Sanyasi Tradition: They are as follows:

1. Vishnu. 2. Kapil 3. Parashar 4. Shounkadi 5. Atri 6. Bhrigu 7. Vamdev 8. Markandey 9. Vyas 10. Kaushik 11. Angira 12. Javali 13. Bhardwaj 14. Shuk 15. Gautam 16. Vashishtha 17. Gandhacharya 18. Balgovindacharya 19. Shankaracharya 20. Padampadacharya 21. Totakacharya 22. Hastamalkacharya 23. Sureshwaracharya.

Shankaracharya established four temples in four directions of India and appointed his four disciples in four directions.

East—Govardhan Math-Jagnathpuri (Orissa). Padmpadacharya.

West-Sharda Math—Dwarka (Gujarat). Sureshwaracharya.

North-Jyoti or Joshi Math: Haridwar (Badrikashram. U. P.). Totakacharya.

South—Shringeri Math; Rameshwaram (Tamilnadu). Hastmalkacharya.

After the death of Jagad Guru Shankaracharya, these four shrines Acharya (Guru) they were decorated as Shankaracharya. Till today these four's chieves are regarded as Shankaracharya (Sharma, 2039 72). Alongwith these four disciples there were ten disciples also. These ten disciples were weak in discourse, so they were not selected as Shankaracharya. They were selected as Dasham Tilak. So they were categorized as Grihastha Sanyasis. Those who could not become Acharyas, they were Giri, Puri, Bharati, Van, Parvat, Sagar, Titha, Ashram, Arnya and Sarswati.

Surnames of Dashnami Sanyasi were determined like this. According to devotional doctrine and worshipping traditions their surnames were determined. Those who reside on the mountains and achieve Tatwa Gyan (Essence of Knowledge) they are called Giri. Those who are full of essence of Knowledge they are called Puri. Those who understanding the essence of learning and renounce the burden of sorrow, they are called Bharati. Those who are far away from their birth and receive essence of knowledge, they are called Van. Those who reside on the top of mountain and receive Atm-Gyan they are called Parvat, those who reside on the seashore and receive Atm Gyan, they are called Sagar, those who reside on the confluence of rivers and receive Atm Gyan, they are called Tirth, those who live in Arnya van (forest) and receive Atma Gyan they are called Arnya, those who live in Grihashthas Ashram and free from the bondages of attachment, they are called Ashram and those who study the

Vedas and Vedic books they are called Sarswati (Puri 1999. 580).

There is also different conception prevalent about the origin of Dashnami. Puri has been originated from the third eye of Shankar, Bharati originated from forehead, Sarswati originated from toungue, Giri originated by shoulder, Van was originated from armpit and, Tirth and Ashram were originated from foot.

Jangam is also associated with Sanyasi tradition like Dashnami who reside in Nepal. They follow the tradition of Shaivism but they are not in Dashnami group. Shaiva Brahmin of South India, Karnataka started this tradition in twelveth century. (Chhetri and Khatiwada). Thus Jangam tradition developed after Dashnami tradition. They do not believe in rebirth and also they do not believe in discrimination. But there is vast similarity between the two traditions. There is also matrimonial relation between the two, (Sharma 2039, 73)

Jangams are also the matrons of many temples. They also act as priests in many shrines, They also maintain and worship daily in so many temples such as Ram Janaki temple of Janakpur, Dattatreya of Bhaktapur, Palanchouk Bhagawati of Sindhupalchouk and Swargadwari of Pyuthan and Indreshwar of Panauti.

Julaha

A community of weavers. The etymology of the word Julaha is from the Persian word Julah, meaning a ball of thread (Rose, 1919) about people commonly associate the word Julaha with Jula or Juli (network of thread).

They go from one home to another in winter season to make mattresses of cotton. They make it according to the choice and demand of the people.

Kahar

(Risley 1891) describes the Kahar as a large cultivating and palanquin bearing caste. They claim their descent from

Jarasandh, king of Magadh. Kahar is derived from the words Kandh and bhar, i.e., one who bears a burden on his shoulders and they are traditional palanquin bearers Mehtar. Referred to under the generic term, Mehtar, their community name is derived from the word hela, meaning a cry. Their typical dress and ornaments as well as tattered marks are their identification marks. They are non-vegetarians who take pork. They are divided into a number of exogamous gotras. They acquire mates through mutual negotiation. The vermilion mark, bangles, bindi, earrings and nose-ring symbolize the married status of a woman. Their girls are married when they are sixteen years old and boys between twenty and twenty two years. Divorce and re-marriage are permissible. Post- marital residence is patrilocal and the traditional pattern of the mixed extended family type is maintained. The rule of inheritance is male equiganiture. " (K. S. Singh: 2010. P. 591).

Their Gotra is Kashyap. They have been categorized as Shudra. They prefer early marriage because they are not very educated. Child marriage is in vogue since very long time but now they prefer and practice adult marriage. They observe monogamy in their community. Mutual consent is a must for marriage negotiation. Vermilion in the forehead and red bangles in the wrist are the symbols of married women. They engage themselves in agriculture during rice plantation and harvest. Carrying palanquin on the occasion of marriage is their main duty. They also carry diseased persons in their palanquin during emergency hour to the nearby health center and village hospital. They also carry brides and grooms during the rainy season. But now adays people use Jeeps and cars on the occasion of marriage. So their traditional occupation is in danger. They are the followers of Hinduism in their daily life. Their favourite Goddess is Lakshmi who is the Goddess of wealth. Goddess Kali is their village deity.

They ferry bride and groom across the river during rainy season. They also carry emergency patients to nearby health centers in villages. So they are very useful caste. They make themselves palki (palanquin) of wood for this purpose in Terai areas.

Deepak Chaudhary writes about this caste in the following lines:

> "The Kahars found in the mid-tarai and western Tarai are socially and economically privileged. Doing physical labour has become their major occupations. In the past, they used to carry Doli (a wooden structure to carry bride or bridegroom) during marriage and do other works of service for the people. They use Kahar as their surname. " (Deepak Chaudhary:2010. P. 97).

Kaibartha/Kaibarta

A fishing community-The word Kaibarta is derived from Ka, meaning water, and varta, meaning lively hood. About Kaibarta, Risley (1891) writes that they are a large fishing and cultivating caste of Bengal proper, ranked below the Nava-sakha or a group of nine castes from whose hands Brahmans take water.

'It is believed that Kewarta word came from 'K' means water and 'Warta' means existence. They are famous as fisherman in Assam and have been farming in Bengal. Relating to fishing, they came from Brahmaputra valley. '(Singh, 2002).

Deepak Chaudhary writes:

> 'Some Kewrata reside in Jhapa, Sunsari and Morang districts in a few numbers scattered on different places. They belong to Indo-Aryan family. ' (Deepak Chaudhary 2010, P. 193.)

But some Kaibarta caste people reside in Sarlahi, Mahottary, Dhanusha, Siraha, Saptari and Sunsari, Rautahat, Bara and Parsa also.

Kalar

This caste has also deep rooted Hindu caste based origin. The very word is considered as derogatory in Maithili language. This caste represents the people who eat things in mannerless and indecent way which is unusual. General people are not accustomed to this behaviour. So people do not take it in a nice way. They have no good social status in the Madheshi community. On the basis of behavioral tendency towards eating food items, the word has been coined. They have ancestral profession of begging for food items and cash for their livelihood. The NDC has listed Kalar as sueparate castegroup. But Terai Madhesh of Nepal (2011) Status of Terai Dalit (2006), Ethnographic study of Terai Dalit (2006) National Dalit Strategic Report (2002) are silent about this caste. The total population of this caste is 1,077 according to 2011 census.

Kalwar

This caste is very famous caste among Vaishya community of Tarai- Madhesh. Business is their main occupation. So this caste is supposed to be very rich caste. But this is not true for the whole community. There is rich and poor both in it.

> "They practise community endogamy and avoid marrying within five ascending generations on both the mother and father's sides. Mates are acquired through negotiation. Bride price is paid in cash." (Sherring, M. A. 1971)

Grooms are heavily paid because their parents demand high price for marriage celebration. Now-a-days they are doctors, engineers, professors and government officers. So they demand too much dowry in marriage. Marriage negotiation is solemnized through mutual understanding. They prefer and choose arranged marriage but love marriage is also taking place in this community rarely. Marriage custom has been becoming very expensive affair day by day these days. Marriages are solemnized at the brides home in a pavilion tastefully and beautifully decorated which presents a worth visiting site for onlookers. Married women put vermilion in their foreheads. They also wear red glass bangles to show that they are married. They follow Hinduism as their main religion. Ayodhya is their main sacred centre. They celebrate Dashahara, Diwali, Gobardhan pooja, Chhath folk festivals every year with gusto . They also observe Satya Narain Bhagawan pooja once in a year atleast. A Maithil Brahaman priest performs all religious ceremonies. Mahapatra Brahmin officiates death ceremony. It is customary for the Kalwar community. Banigoraiya is their clan deity. They also worship Ram and Krishna. They equally worship Durga and

Kali goddesses. So they practise all Hindu rites and rituals from birth to death. The ashes and bones of dead body are immersed in the Ganges preferably and nearby rivers. The main marriage ceremony is solemnized with Sindur Dan and Barmala (garland of fresh flowers). The eldest son claims the right of guardianship after the death of father. They accept water and food from the Brahmins, Rajputs, Bhumihars, Kayasthas, Vaishya, Yadavas, Lohar, Sonar, and Koiris except untouchables.

Sherring writes appropriately about this caste in the following lines:

> "They avail of the facilities of education, health and medicine, family welfare, drinking water, electricity, self employment schemes. They are linked with the world through the radio, cinema, extention agencies, political parties and post offices. (Sherring, M. A. 1971).

The population of Kalwar was not recorded in the census of 2001 systematically and scientifically. One research scholar has forwarded the following reasons for this negligence. I would like to quote:

> " Kalwars have different family names such as Sah/Sahu, Jayaswal/ Jaiswal, Chaudhary, Gupta, Bhagat etc.These family names resemble with other castes such as Sudhi, Kanu, Halwai, Teli, and Sonar also have family names as Sah/Sahu; Tharu has family name as Chaudhary, Kurmi also writes Jaiswar and so on. This confuses the people going for census in the villages who neither have enough knowledge of these family names nor probe appropriately to trace out the facts. Instead they use their own judgement(although mistakenly) and put a caste against the name of an individual;
>
> This problem becomes more serious when people from hill origin/ Kathmandu go for conducting census in Terai because of their acute communication problem. The present population of Kalwar is 128, 232 according to census of 2011 but it is still estimated to be over 2oo,ooo.

Origin of Kalwar caste

"They trace their origin to the Rajputs and affix Singh to their names.

They migrated from Rajasthan during the Mughal period. Now distillation of liquor is their primary occupation."

This might be true that they migrated from Rajasthan but it is wrong to say that their primary occupation is distillation of liquor. They are business men by nature and by schooling also but they are not industrialis. Even they can do small business. But now a days they are doctors, professors, engineers and government servants. They are well known names in active politics. Rameshwar shah and Deodhari Prasad Kalwar were assistant ministers. Radha Krishna Prasad and Vishwanath jaiswal were members of Parliament. Chanda Chaudhary was the assistant minister for youth and sports in the ministry of Madhav Kumar Nepal.

Deepak Chaudhary writes in his book 'Tarai/Madhes of Nepal' about Kalwar in the following lines:

> There is no Gotra among the Kalwars except same using Kashyap. They do not have the system of Bratabandha, some of them are performing it now a days. Among them, there is Baan instead of Gotra. Altogether they have three hundred and sixty five Baans and relation is found out from the main Baan. The same Baan is taken as belonging to the same Gotra. That's why marriage does not take place within the same Baan. In this ethnic group, in case if any dispute or problem, they have managed Chaurasi Sabha(eighty four assemblies) for the solution and it does not exist now. Each of the Sabhas (assemblies) is given a particular area and it solves the problem of the same area via assembly. " (Deepak Chaudhary 2010, P. 87)

> Kalwars consider themselves as the children of Balbhadra. Balbhadra is also called Balram. About Balram It is written in the book named The Gods of Hindus-" It sounds to reason to have Balram with the plough to come and change the way of life of the people of this earth where humanity had multiplied and food got naturally from the forest, was running out. Some one had to find out ways and means to grow food by working at it. Balram was born to teach the people how to dig the earth and put in seeds and produce food in good quantity, and grow it where they wanted it thus making the settlements secure. Balram although holds the plough and is still today acknowledged god as the eighth Avatar, yet he is not much talked of nor the use of the plough stressed. His younger brother Krishna has slowly usurped his position and is

more or less acknowledged as the Avatar. " Om Lata Bahadur: The Gods of the Hindus. Page 127.

Lord Krishna and Balbhadra were brothers. Subhadra was their sister. Balbhadra's wish was to get Subhadra to be married with Duryodhan but Krishna was not in favour of this proposal. He preferred Arjun. So the marriage of Subhadra was solemnized with him. The Byahut branch of Kalwar is very important in the Kalwar community. They worship Balbhadra as their favourite god since the time of the Mahabharat. To day all the Kalwars have age old tradition of worshipping Balbhadra as their ancestor. They consider themselves as his direct descent. They are proud that they belong to the gracious and famous dynasty of Kshatriya. They have been categorized as Vaishya in the caste hierarchy of Hinduism. They have five sub-groups such as Byahut, Kharidaha, Jayaswal, Jayasar and Kalal. Marriage ceremony is equally solemnized among these subgroups but it was not permitted in previous times. Byahut branch of Kalwars are supposed to be the oldest one and they worship Balbhadra Bhagawan with respect and reverence every year. Now the all Kalwars are worshipping him without any feeling. They worship him on the auspicious occasion of marriage with devotion and dedication. They also worship on the beginning of any business. They use the surnames of Shah, Sah, Sahu, Gupta, Bhagat, Prasad, Singh, Chaudhary and Jayaswal. They have good literary tradition. Kashi Prasad Jaiswal and Bhawani Bhikshu were two literary Jiants in this community. Kashi Prasad Jaiswal was a famous historian. Bhikshu was a renowned poet, story writer and novelist of Nepali literature. He was the winner of prestigious Madan prize for his outstanding novel Aagat.

The total population of this caste according to the census of 2011 is 128,232.

Analysis of above population data:

The population of Kalwar is reported to be 128,732 in which the number of male is 28, 703 and the number of female is 99,523.

There are 125 indentified castes/ethnic groups and the number of unidentified others is 15277 and the number of foreigner is 6,651 according to its reported population size (128, 732). The proportion of Kalwar is 0.51 per cent of the total population of Nepal (26,494,504). This can be an indication of Kalwar settling firstly in this part of earth presently divided by border lines between Nepal and India and from here it spreads to east, west and south but not much in the north.

It is interesting to note that there is gradual decrease of population of Kalwar on both sides e.g. east and west of Rautahat district. A similar trend is also observed along our east-west border in India.

Education Status

The education status of Kalwar shows that 65% of Kalwar population is literate. Kalwar comes at number 22 out of 100 castes categorized by Dr. Harka Gurung. Some of the castes that have higher percentage than Kalwar are Madwari, Kayastha, Bahun (hill), Brahmin (terai), Rajput, Baniya, Dev and Chhetri where education percentage varies from 91% to 66%.

Kalwar falls on 31 out of 125 identified castes according to its reported population size(128,732).

The population of Kalwar is recorded to be 128,523 (C.B. C.). This figure may be questionable in itself but this being the only reported data, we are compelled to take it as reference.

Social Status

Social status of Kalwar is neither very high nor very low. According to caste wise social stratification, Kalwar is supposed to be superior to some other castes and inferior to some others, Kalwar does not accept water and food from some castes like, Tatma, Paswan, Dhobi and Dusadh etc and at the same time some other castes like Brahamin, Yadav, Nunia and Hajam etc, do not accept water and food from Kalwar. (M. L. Jaiswal, Kalwar, 2011 P. 117).

Change is the salt of life. According to C.D. Lewis human values are in a melting pot. Human values are changing very fast. So the traditional values are also changing very often.

The social pattern is changing accordingly. Social customs are also changing in the present context that is but natural. There are so many reasons. Urbanisation is one of them. Migration, education, remittance and improved income status and easy penetration in the media world are some of the main reasons. Delivery of social service also causes the status quo of general people.

Economic Status: Change is also taking place in the economic condition of Kalwar caste like in other castes. According to one scholar this changing trend can be interpreted in the following lines:

> "Kalwar also represents different economic categories like landless, poor, medium and rich. Agrarian population is mainly poor to medium though there are some rich people in the rural villages having large land holdings. The landless and poor sectors of the population earn their livelihood as labour force either in the locality of their habitat or in towns/ cities of Nepal and/or India. Some individuals are also working abroad. Some Kalwar families are economically well established and are running high volume businesses. They are supporting the government by providing considerable amount of revenues in the form of income taxes. " (M. L. Jaiswal. Kalwar 2011. P. 120).

Political Status

Political status of this caste in the national level is not satisfactory. This caste is primarily a business class caste. So the people of this caste are mainly involved in business profession. They are syphoning a lot of money to the other caste people in each and every election but they are not coming in the forefront themselves to fight election. This is a drawback in this caste. They are actually playing the role of King makers. They know how to earn money but they do not know how to win election. So they are least interested in the field of politics. That's why this caste was not represented by even a single seat in the contituent assembly of 601 members. This was very harassing situation and frustrating too for this caste. In the past however, some very limited individuals had the privilege of representing this caste in the parliament and in the ministries. Kalwar must feel proud of them for their zeal and courage. Four of them who were successful in winning as members of Parliament were late Mr. Radha Krishna Kalwar from Birganj, Parsa, Late Mr. Devdhari Prasad Kalwar from Bagrampur, Bara, Late Mr. Rameshwar Prasad Shah from Piparia, Sarlahi and Late Mr. Bishwanath Prasad jayaswal from Kalaiya, Bara. Among these four, Mr. Devdhari Prasad and Mr. Rameshwar Prasad had become assistant ministers of land reform and forest respectively.

There is a marriage formula for this caste which is considered at the time of Marriage. This is called from A to Z formula which is given here:

A means age of Bride and Groom

B means Beauty and Behaviour.

C means Character and Caste.

D means Delicate.

E means Education.

F means Family Background.

G means Genius.

H means Health.

I means Intelligence.

J means Job.

K means Knowledge.

L means Leniency.

M means Maturity.

N means Nature.

O means Originality.

P means Personality.

Q means Qualification.

R means Reputation & Religion.

S means Smart.

T means Tolerance.

U means Union.

V means Vision.

W means Weakness and Working Style.

X means Xenomenia.

Ymeans Youthfulness.

Z means Zeal.

They worship Balbhadra or Balram as their favourite God. Especially they worship Him on the auspicious occasion of marriage ceremony. He always carries four ploughs in four hands. Plough is essential for cultivation. I am giving here His short biography.

Balram or Balbhadra is the incarnation of Lord Vishnu. His father's name was Basudev. His mother's name was Rohini. His grand father's name was Shursen. His brothers were Sagar, Shath, Durdam, Daman, Shwabhra, Pindarak, Ushinar. His wife's name was Rewati. His son was Nishath. His sisters were Chitra Apasara, Subhadra , wife of great archer Arjun and mother of Abhimanuya. He was the elder brother of Lord Krishna. He was born on the sixth day of dark fortnight of Bhadra. His life history has been mentioned in details in the great epics such as the Mahabharat, Shrimadbhagwat and Haribansh Puran. He was honest and humble in his behaviour. He was not proud. He was also always in favour of justice. His teacher was Sandipini. His Guru was Parshuram. He was not interested in the great battle of Kurukshetra. So he went on to pilgrimage to avoid the great war. So it is clear that he was the peace lover God.

Kapariya-Kaparia

They derive their name from the Hindi word Kapra, meaning cloth. (Crooke 1896) says that Kapariya either means sellers of old clothes or it is derived from the community belief that they were created after the creation of the earth, from the head (Kapal) of Shiva and Parvati. Recently, a synonym for the community, Khunkhuniya Bhat, has been coined by them. They are non-vegetarians.

There is one family of Kapariya, residing in Barahathwa bazaar of Sarlahi district.

> "Kapariya are divided into two sub-groups, namely Braham Bhatta and Rao Bhatta, and the former claim superior status to the latter. They now use Bhatta and Sharma as their surnames. (K. S. Singh, 2010. P. 784).

Kathbaniya

Kathbaniya is mainly a business class people. This caste is in the minority but very famous in the business sector. This caste is scattered all over Tarai / Madhesh but in a few number. This caste is found in several districts of Tarai/ Madhesh such as Sarlahi, Mahottary, Dhanusha, Siraha, Saptari, Sunsari, Rautahat, Bara, Parsa, Rupandehi, Banke and Bardiya. Deepak Chaudhary has written about this caste in the following lines:

> "The Kathbaniya is one of the minority caste groups living in the Tarai region of Nepal. This group at majority is found in Business/ trade centers of Tarai. The settlement of this group in the districts such as Jhapa, Morang, Sunsari, Saptari, Udaypur, Siraha, Sarlahi, Mahottary, Dhanusha, Rautahat, Banke, Bardiya, Kailali, Kanchanpur, Makawanpur, Nawalparasi, etc, are relatively thin in their configurations. The origin of this group is still unknown and nobody has studied about this group. It has resulted into the difficulty in introducing them with certainty. It is so, the further research is necessary to make the concerned subject referentially clear. " (Deepak Chaudhary: 2010. P. 84-85).

People of this caste use surname of Das. Beni Das of this caste of Godaita (Hanuman Nagar Chhapkahiya) V.D.C. has established High school five decades ago. This is the second High school in the Sarlahi District. His son Mauze Lal Das was a successful and famous teacher of his time. He tried his best to make this school as an ideal school in the whole district during his life time. Late Birendra Das was the General Manager of Janak Material Productions Centre, Ministry of Education, Nepal Government one year before.

In this community marriage procedure initiated by the will of the guardians. Child marriage was also in vogue in earlier times but now a days it is not materialized. Priests are consulted for the auspicious occasion of marriage ceremony and they fix the right date for it. Arranged marriage is in vogue. Considerable amount of gifts is given at the time of marriage. Now a days it is not rare that a dowry (tilak) of fancy goods and cash exceeding a few lakh rupees is given by the bride's side. This is customary for solmnization of marriage ceremony. Since they are business men they give and take sufficient cash to show their social status.

Their women's role is restricted to household jobs and social ritual and economic activities. They contribute to the family income by earning their own bread and butter if they are service holders. Now a days they are highly qualified and earn a lot of money by their jobs. They are engineers, doctors, professors and government officials. House wives are restricted to their household works. They are supposed to follow certain restrictions during their pregnancy because this is a very precious period for them.

Sherring, M.A. writes:

> "A woman has to observe certain restrictions during her pregnancy. The first post-birth ritual (Chhatta) is followed by the barahi and tonsure(mundan) ceremonies. They observe birth pollution for fifteen days." (Sherring, M. A. 1971.)

But this is not true to the word. The first post-birth ritual is called Chhathiar not Chhath as mentioned by Sherring. They also observe birth pollution for twelve days only.

According to the census of 2011 their total population is 138, 637.

Kamalapuris

Kamalapuris also belong to Vaishya society. Their settlement is found in several districts of Nepal. They are settled in Sunsari, Mahottary, Dhanusha and Rautahat. They are well settled in Gaur, headquarter of Rautahat and doing business. They have their own organisation of their castes and are in minority. They have published one soveniur in 2065 B.S. The sensus of 2011 has not included it. So its exact number is not known but according to its caste calculation their total number is 4293. This caste has been originated from a small town named Kamalapur of Kashmir which denotes the goddess of wealth. The people of this caste also believe in it. In 2063 B.S. Falgun 24th they formed an organisation in Lahan named Kamalapuri Vaishya Baniya Samaj which later on changed in the name of Kamalapuri Vaishya Samaj (society). Kanahaiya Prasad Gupta was nominated as chairman and Shankar Prasad as general secretary. Deepak Chaudhary has written in his book:

> "In Nepal, the Kamalapuris exist in very small number. They have been found settled in Sunsari (Bhutaha), Mahotary (Matihani), Dhanusha (Khajuri-Mauha) and Rautahat (Gaur). They use the surnames as Shah and Gupta. They identify themselves as kamalapuri Vaishyas. They are jobholders and their level of education is satisfactory. " Deepak Chaudhary:Tarai/ Madhesh of Nepal: P. 90.

Kasaudhans

Kasaudhans are in minority. They are found settled in Nawalparasi-Kapilvastu and Rupandehi districts of Nepal. The headquarter of Rupandehi Bhairahwa is a favourite living place for them. Aditya Narayan Kasaudhan is very famous and welleducated in his community. Deepak Chaudhary has this opinion about this caste. I would like to quote him here:

> "The Kasaudhans are found in the west. Nawalparasi-Kapilvastu is the area of their settlement and they exist as a minority group. " Deepak Chaudhary:Tarai-Madhesh of Nepal: P. 90.

They are Hindus and worship Gods and Goddesses. Marriage is settled on the basis of dowry. They prefer to marry in the U.P. state of India because they are much more educated and rich. Negotiation is the primary mode of acquiring a mate and monogamy is the form of marriage. Lac bangles, vermillion and necklace are the symbols of marriage for women. Dowry is paid both in cash and kind. After marriage, residence is patrilocal. Divorce is allowed but its instance is very rare and remarriage of widow is also in vogue. They distribute their property equally among the sons but the succession mainly depends upon the eldest son.

After delivery, birth pollution is observed and they perform Sastipuja (Chhathihar) and Annaparasan (first feeding ceremony for newly born child). They cremate their dead according to the Hindu rites and rituals. They observe death pollution for thirteen days. They also celebrate Shradha rituals for their dead parents.

> The important changes in their society are an increased age for marriage, introduction of dowry, proliferation of nuclear families, adoption of some Brahmical religious rites in rituals and abolition of puberty rites for girls. Now they are service holders in private as well as in public sectors. Some of them are also engaged in trade, service, and self employment.

Kayastha

The Kayasthas are famous high class caste in Hindu social setup. Generally the term Kayastha belongs to the caste engaging in the profession of reading and writing. (Hindi Vishwakosa).

In a dictionary the word means a Hindu caste working as a scribe. In Nepali dialect the word Kayastha is pronounced as Kaite which means the caste of reading and writing profession or a Vaishya caste belonging to such profession. On the other hand, the word Kayastha indicates its origin from the Greek word Scythian which has taken the present Nepal. (Brihat Sabdakosa.)

In Sanskrit language the word Kayastha is related to Kaya, the body and thus considered as the Paramatma, the Supreme Being.

The Kayasthas have played an important role in the fields of rule and administration. In the Rajtarangani of Kalhan we meet with numerous instances of Brahmanas engaged in the duties of a Kayastha. (Kalhan: Rajtarangini viii).

In Mithila there is a caste named Bhumihara-Brahman. Likewise in the regions of Northern Bihar of India and Eastern and Middle parts of Nepal Tarai (Mithila Region) there lives a caste named Kayastha Baniya, a subdivison of Vaishya

Varna, with the title (surname) of Dasa. But it has been misunderstood that Kathbaniya is a sub -divison of Kayasth. It is a separate caste of Tarei Madhesh.

Bengal province of India is pre-eminently the land of Kayastha. No other province in India can compare with Bengal as regards the number and importance of the Kayastha community. In the sixteenth century (A.D.) Bengal was ruled by a number of semi-independent and independent princes called Bhuiyas, most of whom were Kayastha.

The Brihad Dharma Purana, which gives a true picture of the social organization of Bengal in Medieval times, assigns the place of honour to the Karana or Kayastha and describes him as not only an expert in the art of writing but a skilful administration (Rajyakayeshu Kusala).

Abul Fazal, the author of Ain-i-Akbari, was informed that Bengal now been under Kayastha rule for long centuries, and that even the Palas and Senas were Kayastha. Budhimanta Khan of Navadvip, Kedara Raya of Vikrampur, Pratapaditya of Jessore, Ram chandra of Chandndvip, etc. were all Kayastha in the 16th century (A.D.)

Thus we find the fact that the Kayastha now a caste was a professional class and with the course became a caste as a result of the contributions from different castes.

Deepak Chaudhary has voiced the same and similar view in the following lines:

> "A very long time ago, they were believed as the kings of the past, for the purpose of state management. They used to appoint their own brethren, mentioning as the people for writing and counting and later on the people who did not leave the profession, separated themselves from their original clan of the Kshatriya and appeared In the form of Kayasthas. " (Deepak Chaudhary: 2010. P. 68)

The Kayastha caste people in Terai are addressed as Munim, Lala, and Diwan and Munshi.

Chitragupta is their favourite God and they worship him every year on the occasion of Bhatridwitiya, next day after the festival of lights, Diwali. They are principally pen pusher. So they worship pen on this occasion.

There are some religious views regarding Kayasthas:-Lord Brahma, creator of this universe said laughingly to the person who had emerged out of his body:

'Your name is Chitragupta. You emerged out of my 'kaya'(body), therefore, you have to be known with the name of Kayastha, therefore, you have to be known with the name of Kayastha and live in the world of Dharmraj, keep the record of good and bad deeds of human beings. '

Karna Kayasthas also maintain Panji system like Maithil Brahmin. They are very particular about the marriage of their children. They do not establish blood relationship in the same gotra. Thus they maintain purity of blood in their relation.

Thus it is crystal clear that Kayastha caste has been evolved from very ancient time to modern time. It is very ancient caste and a very brilliant caste.

There are twelve types of Kayasthas: Bhunu (Shreevastav), Suryadhwa, Bishwabhanu (Balmiki), Biryabhanu (Asthana), Char (Mathur), Sucharu (Gaud), Chitra (Bhatnagar), Matiyan (Saksena), Himwan (Ambasta), Charum (Karna), Chitracharu and Atindriya (Kulshrestha).

The Kayasthas are famous high class caste in Hindu social set up. Generally the term Kayastha belongs to the caste engaging in the profession of reading and writing. (Hindi Vishwa kosa, Varanasi, Nagaripracharini Sabha, 1975 A.D. khanda 2. P. 532)

In a dictionary the word kayastha means a Hindu caste working as a scribe. In Nepali dialect the word Kayastha is pronounced as Kaite which means the caste of reading and writing profession or a Vaishya caste belonging to such a profession. On the other hand, the word Kayastha indicates its origin from the Greek word Scythian which has taken the present Nepal. (Brihat Sabdakosa, Kathmandu, Royal Nepal Academy 2 048, P. 200).

In Sanskrit language the word Kayastha is related to Kaya, the body and thus considered as the Paramatma, the supreme Being.

According to Basudev Lal Das the Kayasthas have played an important role in the fields of rule and administration.

In the Rajatarangini of Kalhana we meet with numerous instances of Brahmanas engaged in the duties of a Kayastha. (Kalhan: Rajtarangini viii 2383 vii 1106).

In Mithila there is a caste named Bhumihara-Brahmana which is comparable with the sentiment of Kayastha Brahman. Likewise in the regions of Northern Bihar of India and Eastern and middle parts of Nepal terai (Mithila Region) there lives a caste named Kayastha Baniya, a subdivision of Vaishya Varna, with the title surname of Dasa. But this is a separate caste.

There is another religious text, entitled Chitragupta Katha, which deals with the origin of the Kayastha caste. According to this text, all the Kayastha sub-castes (Srivastava, Mathur, Saxena, Bhatnagar, Gaur, Karna and Ambastha) are the children of Lord Chitragupta, who himself emerged out of the light of wisdom that emanated from the body of Lord Brahma – the creator of this universe. The Kayasthas not only believe in this text but also worship Lord Chitragupta once a year on a fixed date of the Hindu calendar, i. e., on the second day of Shukla Paksha (moon rising period) of the month of Kartik (roughly November). From the Kayastha point of view, those who have originated from Lord Brahma's light of wisdom cannot be impure or less pure than any other caste. (Gaurang R. Sahay P. 117.)

Bhuiyas are also found settled in Bangladesh.

Budhimantra Khan of Navadvip, Kedara Raya of Vikrampur, Pratapditya of Jessore, Ram Chandra of Chandndvip etc. were all Kayastha in the 16th century A.D.

One Nepali scholar Basudevlal Das has this view about Kayastha caste:

> Thus we find the fact that the Kayastha now a caste was a professional class and with the course of time became a caste as a result of the contributions from different castes. (Basudevlal Das. 2001).

The total population of this caste is 44,304 according to the census of 2011.

Keot

Risley (1891), Buchanan (1891) writes that the Kevats of Bihar and the Kaibatha of Bengal belonged in the earliest times to an aboriginal tribe bearing the name of Kewat. The wealthier and more educated among them consider their brethren in the rural interior areas as not equal to themselves. The Keot have a number of clans, namely Kashyap, Palashi, Nagrashi, Shankharashi, and Anrashi, Dhiber is used as a surname.

Another scholar K.S. Singh writes about Keot in the following lines:

> "They are also referred to as Kevot, meaning fishermen, and are found in several districts of Nepal and West Bengal of India. " (K. S. Singh. The Scheduled Castes.)

The mention of Keot has been made in the Ramayan , the great epic of Hindu. He ferried Lord Ram, Sita and Lakshman while going to forest in banishment and washed His leg. There is another episode also in the Mahabharat. According to which Eklavya wanted to make Dronacharya his guru for archery. But he refused outrightly to make him disciple because he belonged to a lower caste. He, being desperate, built a statue of Dronacharya and practiced rigorously. This way he became expert in archery. Later on when he came to know his expertise in archery, he tried to test his dedication. So he asked for his thumb for Guru Dakschina. He readily agreed and cut of his thumb and gave it to him. Thus Eklavya is remembered for his sacrifice , dedication and devotion. Since then Keots consider themselves as the children of Eklavya. Tulasi Das has described Keot in his great epic Ramayan when Rama started going to the forest along with Lakshman and Sita. They met him on the way. He gave big hospitality to them and showed loyality to them. The great poet Tulasi Das has described it in the following lines:

Keot kinh bahut sewakai/so Jamini singraur gawai.

Hot prat batchhiru mangawa/jata mukut nij sis banawa.

This has been translated like this:

"Guha the boatman showed them great hospitality and the party spent that night at Singraur (Shringaverapura); at daybreak they sent for the milk of the banyan and the two brothers coiled up their matted hair into a crown. Then Rama's friend (Guha) called for a boat, and after putting Sita on board, Raghunatha himself embarked. Lakshman then set his bow and arrows neatly in their proper place and with the Lord's permission also went on board. " (Tulasi Das: Ayodhyakand:P. 344).

According to the census of 2011 the total population of Kewat is 153,772.

Khatwe

This caste is very labourious caste of Tarai-Madhesh. No sociological study has been carried out uptill now of this caste. So it is very difficult to trace out its origin in the true sense of the term. The people of this caste claim themselves as an indigenous one. It means this caste is very old one. The people of this caste are considered as the carriers of palanquin on the occasion of marriage in Terai-Madhesh. They are also very useful people because they use to carry sick people to nearby health center for treatment during emergency. They are also very useful during rainy season when there is no good road. They also ferry unable and disabled people across rivers when there is flood

Mythology: Sashiya Maharaj and his mother Maiyya were regarded as their ancestors. Maiyya Maatair of Ujjain, a city of Madhyapradesh (India) was famous devotee of Indra, Lord of rain. So she was blessed with three kids. They were Sashiya Maharaj, Nikujia and Chiraijii Maharaj. They were considered to be very brave. One of the ancient kings, Darbhanga Maharaj (king) wanted to punish the people of Khatwe community. He put them in Bailsar jail. The people of Khatwe community requested Maiya Maatair for help. So Maatair ordered his son Sashiya Maharaj to help them. He made them free. King of Darbhanga felt ahamed of this event but he made a temple with statue of Sashiya Maharaj in the compound of his palace. The very temple is still in existence. The family members of the king of Darbhanga worship and sacrifice sheep there. According to one study:

"Darbhanga Maharaj accepting the defeat, built a temple with statue of Sashiya Maharaj within the premises of his Palace. According to Ram the temple is still there and the descendants of Darbhanga Maharaj worship Sashiya Maharaj by sacrificing sheep." (NNDSWO: 2006. p. 71.).

Deepak Chaudhary writes about Khatwe in the following lines:

> "Their settlement is found especially in eastern Madhesh. Morang to Sarlahi district in majority. Very long ago, it is believed that this group used to carry Doli (palanquin) during marriage but later on they were deprieved of that work. They are engaged to the work of stitching clothes and doing physical labours and use the surnames as Mandal, Khanga and Khatwe. Some of them are educated but in negligable number. Most of them are landless. " (Deepak Chaudhary: 2011. P. 136)

The total population of Khatwe according to the census of 2011 is 100,921.

They use surnames of Sharma, Kahar, Kapur, Chaupal and Khatri except Mandal and Khanga.

They accept cooked food from many castes except Chamar, Dushadh, Dom, and Halkhor castes.

According to the National Dalit Strategy Report, 2002.

> "Though Khatwes are untouchables, they regard themselves superior to groups such as Chamar, Dushadh, Dom and Halkhor and do not accept cooked food and water from these groups. "

According to another study there is caste based discrimination against this community which is given here:

> "They were not permitted to share the common resources like drinking water with other caste/ethnic groups. They accepted food and water from other communities but hardly any communities accepted from them. " (NNDSWO 2006. P. 76).

But now this is not the case. They are treated equally. There is no such discrimination now a days.

Their women are not educated at all. They are house wives. They cook food daily. They collect and fetch firewood for cooking purpose. They look after their children. Their children do not attend any schools but now a days some of them are enrolled in village schools. Dropout rate is very high.

They had their own village council. The head of it is called Manjan who generally decides the disputes quite often. I would like to quote here:

> "Like other Terai Dalit groups in the study area, they had their own councils. They had their own traditional leaders called as Maijan. He belonged to the same community and was responsible for settling disputes and taking decisions on community affairs. He was chosen by the Khatwes themselves. " (NNDSWO:2006 P. 75).

Their gotra is not Kashyap but Tirhutiya, Bagdaha, Kayota, Parsa Pokharbhinda, Hasuliya, Pusadi and Nanuada. They have their own priest for performing rituals from birth to death. They are mostly non-vegetarian. Their staple food includes rice, pulse and vegetables. They love to eat mutton, chicken, pork, and fish.

Risley (1891)- describes the Kahar as a large cultivating and palanquin- bearing caste. They claim their descent from Jarasandh, king of Magadh. Kahar is derived from the words Kandh and bhar, i.e., one who bears a burden on his shoulders and they are traditional palanquin bearers Mehtar. Referred to under the generic term, Mehtar, their community name is derived from the word hela, meaning a cry. Their typical dress and ornaments as well as tattoo marks are their identification marks.

Koeirs

"The Koeris in the villages call themselves Kushwahas, believing that they are descents of Kush, the second son of Lord Rama. Since Lord Rama and his son Kush were Suryavanshis, the Koeris believe that they belong to the same lineage. As Suryavanshis of the lineage of Lord Rama, the Koeris argue that they have never been involved in polluting occupations and have always followed a pure style of life characterised by vegetarianism and truthfulness. They argue that they have performed the Kshatriya role quite successfully. They cite the establishment of the Maurya Empire as an example to subsantiate their belief, claiming that they are a pure caste, no less pure than anyother caste, and with a distinct identity." (Edit. Dipankar Gupta: Gaurang R. Sahaya: P. 119).

Koeris are now popular as Kushwahas in Nepal and India. They have changed their titles because of education. They are now very prominent caste of Tarai and Madhesh. They were generally under stood as cultivators of vegetables. Their main profession was cultivation of vegetables. But now they are highly qualified and occupy higher posts in private and public sector. They are very active in the political field of Tarai/ Madhesh. Deepak Chaudhary writes in his book Tarai/ Madhesh of Nepal about Koeris in the following lines:

"In Tarai, the ethnic group that grows vegetables is called Koiri. But among them, the educated ones prefer to writ Kushwaha. The Kushawahas consider themselves as the children of Kusha, the son of Lord Rama, and say that Kushwaha comes from the word Kush. " (Deepak Chaudhary:2010. P. 83).

According to the census of 2011 their total population is 306,393.

Kumhar

"The traditional people engaged in making urns out of earth are the potters (kumhar or kumhal in Madhesh) called Kumhars. They use the surnames as Pandit and Sharma. "(Deepak Chaudhary 2011, 97).

The population of Kumhar is 121,196 according to the census of 2011. This number is confusing because it has been mentioned Kumal. In this case Kumhars which are resident of Tarai Madhesh are missing in the present census which is unfortunate.

Kusbadiyas

Their settlement is found in Banke and Bardiya districts in the Bheri Zone. They have no historical record. They are quite different than other castes. They are of nomadic nature. Now they are found settled in Purauni and Manikapur VDCs. Dr. Rajesh Gautam and Asoke K. Thapa have Done study about this caste. According to them:

> "These Kusbadiyas claim descent from the royal line of the Pattharkut Thakurs. Due to their extremely low population, they have remained as a single tribe though there are many gotras within. Some examples are: Koti, Matauram, Utwar (Udhwar), Sohanda, Shekut, Bhaise, Bhuniya, Purbiha, Panchaha, etc.

There is no mention of this caste in the census of 2011.

They fall in the category of Terai/ Madhesh castes because they speak Awadhi language as their mother tongue.

Lohar

They are a traditional ironsmith community. The word Lohar is derived from loha, meaning iron. Hindi is used for inter-group communication. Their life-cycle rituals are performed by a Brahmin priest. Birth pollution lasts for thirteen days and a purification is performed. Pollution ceases after drinking cow's urine. The child is named after consulting a Brahman. Tonsure is performed for male children by the mother's brother (Mama). The sacred thread is put on only at the time of Marriage. (K. S. Singh. 2010. P. 802.)

But Lohars of Nepal do not put on sacred thread because they have been categorised in O.B.C.

There is still controvercy going on whether they are O.B. C. or indigenious nationalities. Some of them are in favour of

O.B.C. where as some of them object it. So they are in between. They are occupational castes. They are given priority at the time of cultivation. They are hired on annual basis for which they are paid in cash and kind. Sometimes a piece of land is given to them for cultivation instead of wage.

They are also called Badhai because they are also engaged in woodworks. They make furniture for the households of people of all standard.

"In Tarai, the Lohars are also called Paunipasari. 'Paunis, in the proper sense of the term, belong to only five castes (Nau, Dhobi, Lohar, Bari and Mallah) because they are paid for their services at fixed points of time in a year. Some Chamars, Paneris, Kahars and Dusadhs also act as Paunis by performing their traditional caste occupations, but are paid the required wage, depending on the services they provide, when the work is done. " (Gaurang. R. Sahay: P. 133.)

In the past, the prosperous caste groups used to keep the professional caste groups in their village giving them some land to build the house and they had to serve the village with their profession. In return, certain amount of money or food grains was given to them annually or half yearly. In Tarai, it was called Paunipasari. " Deepak Chaudhary: Tarai/ Madhesh of Nepal: P. 94.

They profess Hinduism and worship mainly Hindu Gods and Goddesses. Their favourite God is Vishwakarma whom they worship annualy with fan and fair. Besides Vishwakarma they also worship Satya Narayan Bhagwan on many auspicious occasions such as Tilak, marriage ceremony, Nawah and Astayam. I would like to quote here:

> "Marriage rituals are performed according to Vedic rites and the clan is worshipped. The bride and the bridegroom circumbulate the sacred fire on a platform (Vedi) at the bride's place and a Pipal tree at the groom's place. The consumation of marriage takes place on the next auspicious day. The dead are cremated and the mortal remains are immersed in the Ganga at Haridwar. Death pollution

lasts for fifteen days. The priest (Acharya) performs ancestor worship and takes death offerings (Pinddan). (K. S. Singh. 2010. P. 803.)

They use the surnames of Sharma, Thakur and Vishwakarma.

The very word Badhai is supposed to be originated from the Sanskrit word Baradhika, which means cutting of the roots of Barad tree. Now a days there is no vast difference between Lohar and Badhai because both of them have taken the same occupation. Their main profession is to make Hal out of wood, cot, chauki, chair, table, desk, blackboard , bullock cart and tyre. Bullock cart and tyre are very useful means to carry men and materials in the rural areas. So it is clear that this caste is very useful and skilled. They also prepare furniture and sell it in the local market. Their second important occupation is cultivation.

The settlement of this caste is found from Mechi to Mahakali. There are two sub-groups of this caste which are called Pachpidhiya and Jhampal. They are well settled in Sisautia V.D.C. of Sarlahi district. Some of the people of this caste migrated to Barahathwa Bazar in search of green pasture because they are also market minded people. According to the census of 2011 their total population is 101, 421.

Ram Bhakta Thakur of this caste became an ambassador to Egypt and Mr. Gopal Thakur was the member of constituent Assembly and Mrs. Dr. Usha Thakur is the Professor of Hindi literature at Tribhuban University.

Still the attitude towards education is not very encouraging. Monogamy is the tradition. The vermillion mark on the forehead, glass and lac bangles, and veiling the head and face from certain kin and outsiders are the signs of married woman. Birth pollution lasts for six days. Sasthi is observed on the sixth day. Adult marriage is the rule but marriages are arranged through negotiation. Remarriage and divorce are allowed. Widow marriage is also permitted. They do not marry their blood kin and line-age members. They prefer early marriages but now a days this is not in use. Dowry payments are done in cash and kind. Sons share their father's property in equal measure. Succession is in the male line. Women, especially the married ones, have especific economic role in society. According to the census of 2011 their total population is 101,421.

Majhi

They have derived their name from rowing boats, which is their traditional occupation. In Bengal, Majhi means the man who steers a boat or a ferry man (Russell).

Though traditionally they are boat rowers, now business and contract work constitute their source of income. (K.S. Singh: 2010. P.)

They are ancient caste living in Madhesh since many centuries. They are very similar as Mallah and Kewat. They row in rivers most of the time. They are very sturdy and stout in the sense that they do their work even in rainy season. They ferry men and women across river and take wages from them because this is the source of their income. Their economic condition is not very sound.

Deepak Chaudhary writes about this caste in the following lines:

> "The Majhis, the oldest settlers of Nepal Tarai, have been living from Jhapa to Banke districts. They reside in Jhapa and in Chitwan in majority. Their settlements are found in Kumarkhod, Chakchaki, Rangiyathan, Sunbari, Birta, and Anarmani of Jhapa. They have been living near the settlement of Rajbanshi and Gangai communities." (Deepak Chaudhary: 2010. P. 190).

Their life is related with river. So they are fond of fish. They prefer to eat fish and meat and drink frequently. "Majhi is actually a term used by the Hill peoples for those people called 'Bote' in the Tarai (not to be confused with Bhote of the Northern border regions). They are also occasionally referred to as Kushar. All are identical, Majhi. Bote and Kushar, they speak one language and follow the same patterns of life." (Dor Bahadur Bista: People of Nepal: P. 142.)

But I have to say that Bote' is not used in any language of Tarai. This word is used in Nepali.

According to the census of 2011 their total population is 83,727.

Mali/Malakar

Risley(1891) wrote about the Mali or Malakar that they are a caste employed in making garlands and providing flowers for the service of Hindu Temples. All Malakars belong to one gotra. Malakar is the surname but presently some of them also use Malakardas.

Their main duty is to sale flowers and also garlands made of fresh flowers. They are also occupational castes. They serve on special occasions such as marriage and poojas (worshipping). They plant flowers in their own garden. They serve the whole village on auspicious occasions. They themselves make malas and deliver them to their clients in village on the occasions of sacred thread ceremony , marriage ceremony and also on the occasion of worshipping of Satya Narayan Bhagawan (God). They are themselves religious minded people. So they worship Goraiya, Andumali, Kalibandi. Their favourite God is Hanuman. They have aesthetic sence. They are simple and gentlemen. They use the surnames of Mali, Bhagat, Bhandari, Malakar and Saini.

Deepak Chaudhary (2010) wrote about the Malis, the people traditionally engaged in the door to door sale of flowers or the garlands of flowers came to be known as the Malis They are found randomly in every district of Tarai. A great number of them are found in Siraha-Saptari districts. They do not have gotra as well.

Marwaris

Marwaris are mainly business community. They have been migrated from Rajasthan state of India to many countries of the world. They have come from Marwar, so they are called Marwaris. Marwar is their homeland. They also came to Nepal several years ago. No certain date has been ascertained up till now. So they are old habitants of Tarai-Madhesh. According to one scholar:

> "The original Marwaris came to Nepal in a time of booming trade and economy, when India's was stagnant. Nowadays those roles have changed and it is India's economy that is booming. Even though many Marwaris are leading the Indian boom in centers like Delhi, Mumbai, Banglore and Kolkata. The Marwaris of Nepal seem content to stay. They see themselves as Nepalese and don't see a stagnant economy as a good enough reason to leave their homes. " (Pat Cauba: Vivacity: Dec. 2011 P. 78).

It is believed that that 40% of Nepal's economy is made by Marwari businesses and businessmen.

Deepak Chaudhary writes about the Marwari community of Nepal in this way:

> "The history of the Marwadis, in Nepal, is nearly of one hunderd and fifty years. Undoubtedly, the Marwadi community started the foundation of industries and factories in Nepal. Even at present they have dominated in the field of industries and import and export tradelinks of Nepal. The well known industrial families of Nepal are represented by the Marwadi community. " (Deepak Chaudhary: 2010. P. 127).

They are very religious minded people and most of them are the followers of Jain religion. The founder of this religion is the First Tirthankar Rishabhdev. Vardhaman Mahavir is the last Tirthankar whose followers are found all over the world. These followers are divided in four major sub groups such as Digambar, Swetambar Murtisiyak, Shwetambar Sthanbasi and Swetambar Terapanthic Dharmasanyash. The followers of this religion use surnames such as Jain, Golchha, Duggad, Vaidya, Sethiya, Dhanawat, Begbani and Sancheti.

Origin: They belong to Marwad of Rajasthan, a state of our neighbouring country India. Therefore they have been named Marwadi. The very word Marwad has been originated from Maruwat, a Sanskrit word, and Maru means Marubhumi.

Legend: Once upon a time Haryana was the kingdom of Agroha. Agrasen was the founder and ruler who was born to the Solar Dynasty. He is their favourite God. Once it so happened that the Goddess Lakshmi came to his house and requested him to adopt the profession of business and to avoid war because his dynasty was mainly related to war. So she suggested him to take the path of peace and hate violence. King Agrasen became the follower of non-violence. He also became very benevolent and compassionate. He also stopped the tradition of sacrificing animals. So he became so popular and was being worshipped by the Marwari Community.

They are still very peaceful community and believer of nonviolence. I once requested late Hulas Chandra Golchha to invest in hotel industry but he did not agree by saying this that in hotels people eat meat and drink liquor. So he outrightly refused my request. It also indicates that they are very religious minded people.

The Marwari community has prominent place in the field of commerce and industry in Nepal. Two Nepalese scholars have this view regarding this community. I would like to quote here their view:

> "The other community which has dominated trade and commerce in the Tarai as well as in Kathmandu is that of the Marwaris. Their influence can be seen mostly in the fast- growing industrial centres along the border. But even Marwaris are beginning to take some interest in the socio-political life of the nation. " (Edit. T.R. Vaidya: B.R. Bajracharya: 1996. Nepal. P. 5).

According to the population survey of 2011 their total population is 51, 443.

Musahar

K.S. Singh (2010) has the following view about the Musahar:

> "The Musahar are divided into exogamous clans (gotras) such as Balakmuni or Balakmun, Daitinia, Sahlaur, Rikhmun, Rishimuni, Tisbaria, Bansghat, Danharie, Sarpurkha, Kasmela, and so on. Majhi, Mandal and Mushar are their surnames.
>
> According to some, the term Musahar (masu meaning flesh, hera meaning seeker) signifies flesh seeker or hunter, and another view

> holds that Musahar (Musa+har) means rat taker or rat eater. They are largely agricultural labourers. The traditional and primary occupation of the community is agricultural wage labourer while the subsidiary occupations are pig rearing, collection of snake skin, and so on. (K. S. Singh 2010. P. 967.)

According to Sir H. Herbert Risley, 'Musahars are an offshoot of the Bhuiya tribe of Chota Nagpur. Arjun Kumar stated that they began to migrate to the paddy-growing plains of Bihar probably since the 12th century and have been the single largest source of agricultural labour in the region ever since (Kumar 2006). It is said that large number of Musahars entered Nepal during Rana regime to cut tree for expansion of Indian railway as well as arable land in the Terai (Jha 1998, NNDSWO 2006).

There are two types of Musahars in Nepal Tarai/ Madhesh namely Tirhutiya and Maghadhiya. According to Madhu Giri , 'Nepalese Musahars were treated and categorised as Tarai Dalits on the basis of relationships between Jamindars and Musahars in Uttar Pradesh. (2012). There is not any particular occupation of Musahars except soil cutting. According to Madhu Giri:

> "Other castes have their own specific ritual occupations and roles in villages. However, the Musahars do not have any ritual occupation. Soil cutting is not ritual occupation, rather it is just labour and people of other castes do practice the same. Their cultural tenets including gender roles are quite similar to Tharu community of the Central-East Tarai and physical appearance is similar to Jhangad and Munda.."

There is a Madheshi poet who has written a beautiful poem about Musahar. I would like to quote here:

> "The horoscope of the nation says
> That anything can happen this year-
> Hailstones may strike the belly of Giridhari Lal
> Or he may make endless money.
> This year harvest may be unexpectedly good
> Or it may experience a terrible draught.
> This year Banarasi Babu may win the election

With the biggest possible margin ever
Or he may suffer an overwhelming defeat.
This year unsocial elements may be very active again
Or they may be cut down to their sizes for ever.
Anything can happen this year.
Yet one thing is certain-
Whether there is a terrible draught or good harvest
Whether Banarsi Babu wins the election or loses it
This year Bhussa Musahar won't sit quietly.
It's upto you to guess
What he will do actually.
Your guess may be hundred percent right
Or it may be hundred percent right
Or it may be hundred percent wrong.
But it may be hundred percent wrong.
But one thing is certain-
This year Bhussa Musahar won't sit quietly!
This year Bhussa Musahar won't sit quietly!!"

According to this poet Musahar is one of the poorest and most exploited tribes from the plains of Nepal. (Shailendra Kumar Singh: Contemporary Nepali Poetry P. 41).

Deepak Chaudhary writes about Musahar in the following lines:

> "Among the Dalits of Madhesh, they form the second largest number after Chamars. Their settlement is found in Morang district in the east and upto Banke district in the west. This group eats various types of meat as the meat of mouse and pig. They take alchoholic things too. Various-sub-groups include Maghaiya, Tirhutiya, Tirausiya, Sinauriya and Kahariya. " (Deepak Chaudhary:2011. P. 133)

They claim themselves to be an indigenous community living in Nepal for thousands of years.

According to some they migrated from Chhota Nagpur plateau of Bihar and have been staying in Nepal for 6-7 generations. They are like Nomads. They are more or less similar to that of the Munda tribe of Chhota Nagpur of Bihar. According to some others Musahars in great number entered

Nepal as wage labourers for clearing the Terai forest during the Rana Regime.

> "Musahars along with other caste/ ethnic groups entered Nepal as laborers to clear the forest. However some of the locals of Hanuman Nagar VDC said, Musahars migrated from Bihar due to the severe drought in 18th century." (NDSWO. 2006 P. 77)

Their local Deity is Dina Bhadri. They profess Hinduism in their life but they are forced to change their favourite religion Hinduism to Christianity due to poverty. There is a popular rhyme in their community which runs like this:

Chati and bhaiya

Runu and Jhunu

Hansraj and bansraj.

There is a myth about this community. I would like to quote.

> "They are believed to be the descendents of Sabari of Risi Kul Samaj of ancient time. According to Hindu epic Ramayana, Sabari was the great devotee of Lord Ram and she offered hospitality to Ram and Laxman while they were searching for Sita, the consort of Ram. Sabari did not have anything to offer excep the bair (a type of fruit) she was eating. She offered the left over a bair to Ram. The hospitality of Sabari made Ram ask her for wishes if she had any. She wished for two sons. After 10 months in a village called Jogiya(jhajhar), Nishu, wife of Kaluram gave birth to the twins. They were named Dina Bhadri and Dina Ram.

Dina Bhadri and Dina Ram are ancestors of Musahars

They both were born in Jogiya (Jhajhar), a village situated in Bihar in the 11th century. It is believed that two brothers used to visit Kataiyya Khab of Saptari district frequently to pass their time during their childhood. They grew up to be renowned wrestlers. In their village there used to be an autocrat named Kanak Singh Dhammi. He used to trouble villagers by forcing them to till his land. The two brothers found out about their parents being forced to till Dhaami's land. They were furious and almost beat Dhaami to death. From then onwards, Dhaami stopped troubling the villages." (NNDSWO. 2006. P. 77-78.)

They worship different village deities such as Kali, Kamala, Kaila, Gagur, Rupa, Maina, Saini Sardar, Panchi Sardar, Chhetri Rangpal, Sursen, Lukenthi, Gaiyya, Param Bir. Dina Bhadri is the most popular among them. They offer puja to him in the month of Jun/July annually and also collectively. They celebrate this puja festival with great fan and fare and for this purpose they collect donation from their community members. They distribute Pan (betel leaf, Supari (Betel nuts) and Khir (rice pudding). There has been no tradition of sacrificing animals and birds. So all villagers take part in this annual celebration very enthusiastically and after this celebration they start planting rice saplings in their already well tilled fields. In other words rice planting ceremony starts formally.

The total population of this caste is 234,490 according to the census report of 2011.

The Musaharas belong to Tarai Dalits caste group, with a total population of 234,490 (CBS 2011). Their settlements are scattered from the east to west Tarai. They are found in Siraha, Saptari, Sarlahi, Sunsari, Dhanusha, Morang, Udayapur, Mahotari, Bara, Parsa, Rautahat, Rupendahi and Nawalparasi districts of Nepal Tarai/Madhesh. Historically, their livelihood strategies have been closely attached to the land(social cutting-information of arable land, pond construction and agricultural labour) but unfortunately land ownership was detatched from them. Socio-economically, more then 96.67% are landless labour (CEDA 2OO7). Their adult literacy rate (7.3%,), female literacy rate (3.8%), life expectancy and position on human development indices are the lowest (2010). Politically, their representation in decision making spheres is almost nil. Though Musahars are significant population size, they were neither elected nor nominated in the Constitutional Assembly in 2008 and more than this none of them elected or nominated VDC chairperson (Giri 2012).

"Musahar' means one who eats rats (Jha1998, Kumar 2006). Mukul sharma cited Hebert Risley's arguments that Musahar literally meant" rat-taker' or 'rat-eater' (from 'musa which means rat and 'har means seeker) or even 'flesh-seeker or 'hunter'(masu means flesh)(Sharma 1999).

According to Arjun Kumar a good number of Musahars do eat rats, as many other tribal groups do. In the post-harvest season, Musahars seem to compete with rats for the leftover/dropped grains in the field. Having done this for centuries, the community has honed up its skill in catching rats unlike other communities. But eating rats is by no means confined to them. What is important, however, is the dehumanizing stigma attached to the community due to this practice (Kumar 2006).

"The Musahar are divided into exogamous class (gotras) such as Balakmuni or Balakumari, Daitinia, Sohlaur, Rikh-mun, Rishimuni, Tisbaria, Bansghat, Danharie, Sampurkha, Kasmeta, and so on. Majhi, Mandal and Musahar are their surnames. "(K.S. Singh: 2010. P. 965.)

Nowadays child marriage is not in vouge but it was in earlier days. They prefer adult marriage. Dowry is given in cash and kind. Married women put on vermilion on their hair parting and wear bangles. They are called Sadhawa with (husband). Widow marriage is allowed. K.S. Singh writes about this caste in the following lines:

> "They are monogamous. Married Women put vermilion (sindur) in their hair parting and wear bangles(lahti). Dowry is given in cash and kind. Post- marital residence is patrilocal. Only the husband can divorce his wife with the sanction of the caste council (Panchayat) on grounds of adultery and for other reasons. " (K.S. Singh: 2010, P. 965.)

Deepak Chaudhary writes about this caste as follows:

> 'It is believed that the Tirhutiyas exist in the largest number among them. Musahars worship Dinabhadrias their family deity. They take Dinabhadri as their great and brave ancestor. Dina and Bhadri were two brothers and they were born in Jogia-jazar village of Saptari district. They were expert in wresling and hunting and had defeated the feudal lords of the region. " (Deepak Chaudhary 2010. P. 134)

According to the census of 2011 the population of Musahar is 234,490.

According to some, the term Musahar (Masu means flesh, har means seeker) signifies flesh seeker or hunter, . There is also another view which states that Musahar means rat-taker or rat eater. They are largely agricultural labourers. The traditional and primary occupation of the community is agricultural wage labour, while the subsidiary occupations are pig rearing collection of snake skin, and so on. (K. S. Singh 2010. P. 967)

They run after field to field during the harvest season to catch rats. They eat the meat of rats. Their children do not enroll into any schools according to a report published by Non-formal education centre and World education. Even Student Enrollment compain undertaken by Unicef, World Education, Aasaman Nepal, Dhanusha Sewa Samiti, Samaj Vikas and community Family welfare Association is not working satisfactorally.

Children from Musahar community pass their time; they have not been admitted to any public schools in the locality. (The Republica daily 22 Dec. 2012.)

According to Gyanu Adhikari

> "Most human rights violations are less 'sensational' than a wartime killing. Take the example of the Musahar children. Through the collective efforts of our bureaucracy and the 'nationalism' of our politicians- many of whom consider a Musahar citizen to be a threat to national sovereignty- there are thousands of Musahars withought citizenship certificate. A Musahar Child born to such a parent can not go to school, since he or she needs a birth certificate to enroll. " Gyanu Adhikari: Depleted potential: The Kathmandu Post: Sept. 11. 2013.

Deepak Chaudhary writes in his book about Musahar in the following lines. I would like to quote:

> "Especially in Terai, the Musahars dig the field for farming and they are well-known for feeding on rats. They were called Musahars for the same region as some people believe. Most of them do not have their own land. Among the Dalits of Madhes, they form the

> second largest number after Chamars. Their settlement is found in Morang district in the east and up to Banke district in the west. This group eats various types of meat as the meat of mouse and pig. They take alchoholic things too. Various sub-groups include Maghaiya, Tirhutia, Tirausiya, Sinauria and Kahariya. " (Deepak Chaudhary: 2010 P. 18)

Dinabhadri is their village deity whom they worship annually with great pomp and show. Most of them speak Maithili, Bhojpuri and Awadhi languages and so the word 'mus' means rat in these languages. So their very origin is Madheshi and not Nepali as Deepak Chaudhary has stated. They have no Nepali connotation in their origin. There is no need of Nepalisation of origion of the Musahar community.

Mythology: Dina and Bhadri were two brothers. They were born in Jogia-jazar a village in the district of Saptari. They were big wrestlers and hunters in their locality. They were also very famous and popular in their community. They attacked on various feudal states and got victory on them with the help of their loyal subjects. In this way they were known as very adventurous heroes of their time. But unfortunately they were killed under conspiracy. It is believed that they were poisoned by some one. Therefore they have unflinching faith in them and worship them as their ancestors.

They also have the same and similar regard and respect for Kali, Surasain, Lakser, Salhesh Bhuma, Maharaj and Sardar and also worship them every year. Though they have been catagorised as Dalits, still they have faith in Hindu Gods and Goddesses such as Brahma, Vishnu, Mahesh, Lakshmi, Parvati and Kali. They use gotra such as Balkamum, Rishimuni, Tisavariya, Bansghat, Dhanhariya, Sarpurkha kasmera. Their head of the community is known as Mukhiya (Chief). The chieves play very pivotal role in settling ethnic conflict in the community. They do not marry in their blood relations. They avoid at least three generations while settling matrimonial relations. They observe certain festivals on various occasions which are famous in the Hindu religion. Child marriage and polygenic is prevalent in this community because the literacy rate is very low in this community. Widow marriage is allowed. Dowry system is also prevalent. Married Musahar women put on Sari, Saya and blouse. Their married men wear Dhoti, Kurta, Banyan, Golganji and Shirt.

They speak Maithili, Bhojpuri, Awadhi , Bajika and Hindi in their daily conversation. They observe Hinduism as their main religion. But now a days they are compelled to conversion only because of poverty. They observe birth rites and death rites like Hindus.

According to the population census of 2011 their total population is 234,490.

Nuniya

They are related with salt making. Nun means salt in the dialects of Madhesh. They are also popular as Chauhan. One scholar has written about this caste in the following lines:

> "Their community name, Nuniya, is derived from the word nun, meaning salt and they are traditionally saltworkers. The Nuniyas are non-vegetarians who do not eat pork and beef. Rice and wheat are their staple cereals. " (K.S. Singh:2010. P. 1004.)

Deepak Chaudhary's view is like this about Nuniyas:

> "The Nuniyas refer to the ethnic group that digs out salt from the land. Along the invention of the technology of digging out salt with machine, they have been separating themselves from this occupation. They are by and large found to be engaged in digging the soil, working as labourers in the field, digging wells and laying bricks and other works like making. They are also known as Loniyas. " (Deepak Chaudhary: 2010. P. 99.).

They have five subgroups, namely Bachgotra, Chauhan, Audhiya, Kharbat and Beldar. They are Hindus by religion. So they worship Hindu Gods and Goddesses in their homes as well as in temples. I would like to quote here again K. S. Singh:

> "They are Hindus and worship Shiva and Durga as their main God and Goddess. Chhatta, Holi and Durgapuja are the major festivals that are celebrated. Kasi is considered to be a pilgrimage centre. The chatri Brahman is their sacred specialist who performs various

> rituals associated with birth, marriage and death. " (K.S. Singh: 2010. P. 1005.)

According to one scholar Nunias are the direct descent of Prithviraj Chauhan. I would like to quote:

> "Likewise, the Nonias claim that they are Kshatriyas belonging to the lineage of Prithviraj Chauhan, the last Hindu king of Delhi. They believe that their forefathers had opposed the Muslim invaders, particularly Muhammad Ghori, who attacked Delhi and eventually defeated and killed Prithviraj Chauhan. The Nonias were, therefore, suppressed and deprived of their land, their main source of wealth and livelihood in the villages, by the Muslim rulers. That is why, they argue, their political and economic position in society has gone down. This does not mean, however, that they have ceased to consider themselves a pure caste belonging to the Kshatriya varna." (Gaurang R. Sahay: P. 118)

William Rowe has also recorded a similar story provided by the Nonias in his village study (Rowe 1991).

Their total population is 70, 540 according to the population survey of 2011.

Patharkatta

This caste has no permanent residence in any village or town. It is scattered everywhere. In true sense of the term it is wanderer or roamer which runs and roams from one village to another to sell its products. The literary meaning of this Patharkatta is to cut and crush stones. It is very hard work. Pathar means stone and katta means to cut or crush.

The Patharkatta/Kushwadiya is probably the lowest Terai Dalit groups in terms of population size. They numbered 3, 182 in the census of 2011. The patharkatta population with more than 10 can be found in four districts. They seem to be relatively concentrated in western and mid-western Terai region. Banke has the highest Patharkatta population followed by Nawalparasi, Rupandehi and Bardiya. (NNDSWO 2006. P. 85.)

Now a days they are concentrated in urban areas such as Birganj, Nepalganj, Janakpur, Bhairahwa and Biratnagar. There is a good market of their products. Villagers even come and buy their products in good number. They make Jata for grinding purposes. It is a stone slab for grinding spices and wheat. It is light and movable. It is also meant for making pulses or lenitals. So it is very useful for household purposes.

Deepak Chaudhary writes about this caste in the following lines:

> "They are found randomly from Nawalparasi to western Bardiya districts. Almost thirty five houses of Kushabandhiya have been living in Indrapur VDC, ward number 3 of Banke district. In this place, they identify themselves as Kushabandhiya. In the past, they used to live in the huts in a very small area of land given by the landlords and their traditional occupation is making ropes (of jute plant, straw or dry grass) and Silauto (a slab of stone for grinding spices)." (Deepak Chaudhary. 2010. P. 143.)

They profess Hinduism in their daily life. They worship Goraiya their clan deity. They celebrate it annualy in the month of Shrawan (July) on the fifth day of the month. They are treated as untouchables. They are allowed neither in teashops nor temples. It is a matter of great regret that though they practise Hinduism yet not they are allowed in the places of pilgrims.

According to one study

> "As mentioned earlier, Patharkattas are nomadic groups who travel from one place to another to sell their products. In the study area, during an interview with one of the Patharkattas, he informed that their traditional occupation is to crush the stone and make different items like silauta (stone item for grinding) and jato (stone item for crushing grains). It was learnt that they entirely depend on this occupation. As they migrate from one place to another quite frequently, they did not have any land of their own. They carry a tent with them and wherever they go, they install it and stay. ' (NNDSWO 2006 P. 88-89)

They move from one place to another with their family members and with a dog which protects them day and night.

Poddar

Poddars are like Marwari and Dev castes. They are similar in so many ways that people are confused sometimes to distinguish among them. They are also called Chaurasi. They are centrally located in the district of Saptari and Sunsari. They are in minority. So they are lagging behind in many fields. Their main occupation is business and culture. This is a separate caste but Poddar is the surname of the Marwari community.

Rajbhars

"The Rajbhars believe that they belong to the Khastriya varna because they constitute a sub-caste of the Rajput. They claim that they too are Raghuvanshis belonging to the linage of king Raghu. They argue that the difference between them and other Rajputs is not a caste difference but a class one. " (Gaurang R. Sahay. P. 118).

This has been mentioned in the Oxford History of India (8th. edition) in the page 91-92 that the Rajputs of Awadh dynasty are related to the caste of Bhar and they are the descendent of Bhar. Now they are considered backward.

The French writer Buchanan Hamilton has written in his book Kingdom of Nepal that their settlement is in eastern and mid- terai of Nepal. Though they are very ancient caste but they are not progressing in the field of education as well as in economics.

Deepak Chaudhary writes in his book named Tarai/ Madhesh of Nepal about this caste in the following lines:

> "The Rajbhars do not hold a big population. A well- known saying about them is that the ancient king of this dynasty was true devotee of Lord Shiva and as he carried the token of Shivalinga (the phallus of lord Shiva) , He was addressed as Bharshiva. Later on, the very Bharshiva was known as Bhar and after a very long time it became Rajbhar." (Deepak Chaudhary: 2010 P. 91).

One scholar has accepted that they have marriage relationship with Rajputs. I would like to quote here again:

> "The Rajputs maintain the difference because they occupy a higher position in the agrarian economic structure. However, they assert that rich Rajbhar families have always established marriage relationships with the Rajputs."

According to the census of 2011 their total population is 9, 542.

> "They belong to Kashyap gotra. They use the surnames such as Chaudhary, Singh, Varna, Raya, Sinha and Rajbhar. Their settlement is scattered from Mechi to Mahakali. They are found in Sunsari, Morang, Saptari, Bara, Parsa, Nawalparasi and Banke districts. They are landless people and work as labourers. They have no good education. So they are jobless also."

Sarbariya

Sarbariya caste is very mobile in the sense that it moves from one place to another frequently. It is hybrid caste in the true sense of the term. one scholar has said that every Sarbarya is hybrid child. It is an admixture of several castes. So some scholars have coined new terminology for this caste that is rainbow. It is an interesting garden of many castes. According to some sociologists it is an ocean caste in which different river castes mingled. The people of this caste claim themselves as super and have many inner connection with various vibrant castes. This caste is vagabound and visible in the Madheshi community. It is an outcome of inter caste marriage and very often of love marriage. So the boys and girls of this caste do not have prestigious place in the society. So they make their own community. They are not easily accepted in the society. Sometimes they are compelled to struggle to adjust in the society. This caste is called Biltua in the different languages of Tarai- Madhesh. This very Biltaua terminology is suitable in the society. At the outset these uprooted people were termed as Biltaua and lateron as Sarbariya. Now they have been recognised as a separate caste in the Society of Terai-Madhesh. They have their own visibility everywhere in the society.

In the beginning of 19th century they settled collectively in Raghunathpur V.D.C. of Dhanusha District before that they were wanderers according to one retired engineer named Ram Briksha Shah of this village. Sarbariya caste is quite different from Sarbhang, Halkhor and Kalar castes. According to Shah these castes might have mingled in Sarbariya because of intercaste and love marriages but Sarbariya is not equivalent to any of these castes. They assert themselves that they are completely different from the castes Halkhor, Kalar and Sarbhang. They say that many couples of these castes may have merged and mingled into Sarbariya on the basis of intercaste marriage and exclusion from their own castes.

Sarbariya caste people are same and similar like Hindu people but they have been categorised and classified as Shudra Varna which has very low status in the society. This caste is not very old and considered untouchable. This caste has been included in the Hindu religion. So it is supposed to worship Hindu Gods and Goddesses. As followers of Hinduism this caste worships Hindu gods like Rama and Krishna , Shiva and Goddesses like Durga. Parvati, Bhagawati. This caste has no definite local deity but it is very religious minded.

Sarbariya people speak many languages such as Maithili in the Mithila region, Bhojpuri in the Bhojpuri region and Awadhi in the Awadh region. They Speak Hindi as their link language. Now educated youths can speak Nepali language also. They are mixing with the people of other castes in day to day life. Sarbariya is itself a Hindi word.

Deepak Chaudhary writes about Sarbariya in the following lines:

> "They are the followers of Hinduism and they also have family deities that include Kali, Bhagawati, Bhairava and Goraiya. Worship of Goraiya is performed by the sub-group Ramani. Marriage is restricted among the followers of having the same family deities. They have the tradition of keeping the flag of Lord Hanuman. 'Baba Barakhandi' is worshipped as village deity. The traditions of solicitation and sacrifice of animals also exist among them. (Deepak Chaudhary:2010, P. 142).

According to census of 2011 the population of Sarbariya is 4,906.

Sarbhang

This caste has been coined on the basis of mannerless and detestable eating habit of certain group of people. In the region of Mithila Sarbhang is known as Aghori. This type of people is supposed to be not neat and clean in their daily life. Aghori is the group of people who changes its dress as beggars and it live on begging. It is not a group of nice people. So people hate them and do not have good idea about this group of people. This group is vagabond type of people who has no permanent house to live in. An Aghori is supposed to eat human flesh to live in and it wanders near by cremation sites. He has human skull in which he uses to eat. He is very odd people to look at. He even practices Tantra and Mantra. He uses ash over his body. On the basis of mannerless and detestable eating behaviour of certain group of people, this word has been coined. Sarbhang is known as Aghori. Aghori is the group of people who change their dress to beg food items. This is a Maithili word.

Sudi

Risley (1891) mentions the Sunri, Saundika, Sundaka, Shaha (as) a large and widely diffused caste found in most dists. of Bengal and Behar, whose original profession is believed to be the manufacture and sale of spirituous liquors. Many of its members have now taken to Mercantile pursuits, call themselves by the title Shaha, and discovers all connection with those who still follow the characteristic occupation of the caste.

> "They are also Known as Saundika, Sundika and Shaha. Suri might be a derivative of the Sanskrit word Shaundik meaning a spirit seller. "(K. S. Singh, P. 1244).

They are true followers of Hinduism. They worship Hindu Gods and Goddesses. Most of them are nonvegetarians but they do not eat beef and pork. No Hindu eats beef because it is taboo. Cows are regarded as mothers by Hindus.

Deepak Chaudhary writes in his book about Sudi in the following lines. I would like to quote:

"The main occupation of this ethnic group is farming and beating paddy. The two main branches of this group are Dhaneshwor/ Saghaut and Byahut. The people engaged in farming and beating rice belong to Dhaneshwor likewise those on business belong to Byahut. The Dhaneshwors are large in number. The socio-economic situation of the Sudis is of average. " Deepak Chaudhary. 2010. P. 85-86.

Now their socio-economic condition is improving very fast. Dr. Upendra Mahato of this caste is one of the richest men of Nepal who has his business network in many countries including Russia. The people of this caste are also coming up in the main stream of politics. Raghubir Mahaseth was the minister of irrigation in the ministry of Jhalnath Khanal. His wife Juli Mahaseth was one of the members of last Constitute Assembly.

Like her there were many women members in the constitute Assembly of this caste. It means women are also coming up in the fore front of politics. This is a good sign of progress of this community in every field. Their settlement is mainly consentrated in Tarai- Madhesh districts of Mahottary, Dhanusha, Siraha, Saptari and Sunsari.

"The Sunris are broadly divided into two occupational distinct sub-groups, namely Shaha (not connected with distilling) and Modo Shaha (distillers). They were once endogamous but now intermarry. They are into several exogamous clans, such as Sandilya, Aliman, Kashyapa, Gargarisi, Madgullareti. Earlier they had only one surname Shaha but now many of them have taken Das as a surname. They practise community endogamy and clan exogamy, barring marriage within five ascending generations. Negotiation is the primary mode of acquiring a mate and monogamy is the form of marriage. (K.S. Singh. 2010. P. 1245)

Negotiation is mainly done on the basis of dowry in cash and kind. Widow is allowed to remarry. They spend a lot of money on the occasion of marriage for showing of their social status and standard. This has become fashion in the Madheshi society. But now a days social awareness is increasing in this community and they consider it as a social evil.

In the census of 2001 Kalwar and Sudi were included in one caste Sudi which was blunder because they are separate castes. According to the census of 2011 the total population of Sudi is 93,115. They have been also misspelled as Sudhi which is wrong. Their main occupation is agriculture.

Tatma

They claim themselves as indigenous people of Nepal but little is known about their origin. They used to weave clothes for kings in ancient times on handlooms. They are also expert in making ropes for different purposes. This community derives its name from the word Tan which literal meaning is handloom in their mother tongue. They also claim that they are the descents of Madhukar Das, a Vaishnaivite. Vaishnaivite people in Terai- Madhesh are in Majority. They are the devotees of Lord Vishnu. They are also called Bunkar which means weaver of clothes. Since they are the followers of Madhukar Das, so they worship him annually with great reverence and respect. They generally offer Khir (rice pudding) and Paan (betel leaf) to their beloved God. According to one study there are five different groups of Tatmas such as:

Kanaujiya: Migrated from the place Kanauj, India.

Banaudhiya: Forest dwellers (ban is in their language is forest)

Dhol bajuwa: Those who play dhol (a type of drum).

Magahiya: Migrated from the place called Maga (Madhyapradesh).

Though there were different groups of Tatma there was no hierarchy as such. (NNDSWO 2006. P. 91.)

According to the population census of 2011 their total population is 104, 865.

Teli

"The Teli belong to the occupational caste of oil pressers, but now a days they are taking to other vocations like agriculture, agricultural labour, labour service and business. With the setting up of oil pressing machines the utility of the old methods of oil pressing is declining. " (K. S. Singh: 2010. P. 1252).

The Teli in Nepal have their own strong organisation to look after their alround welfare. They have named it Tailik Kalyan Samaj, Nepal which aims to foster different services to people of its caste by active participation of the same group of people. It is a non-profitable non-governmental social organization. This organization is dedicated to people of caste Teli which works in conjunction to other such organisation. It is a national level organization with its own norms and values. Many sub-organizations in different district level are well established and others are in developing phase. It has manyfold functions in the field of social service especially in times of crisis. Traditionally, when an individual requires financial aid for example at birth, death, sickness, or disaster, members of this organization will render financial aid immediately. It has varying degrees of capacity, depending on the social, political, financial, educational background that this contended with. Many qualified persons such as engineers, doctors, lawyers, businessmen, politicians, social workers etc. are there with their active participation to upgrade the position of their caste in society. Some inns (Dharmashala). Kutties (cottages), schools and many other things are running and they have also future plans and programmes.

I would like to quote here:

" It is a matter of pleasure to know that Teli Samaj is doing a lot to bring the fact in progress and actively involved in developing country as well as society. It would be rather worthy, if works would be individualized and disabled would be uplifted. Team approach would be better thought. It would be shameful to not mention the progress of Telis who used to starve for food and do manual works have scaled a height from hut to Member of Parliament. Education has enlightened our life and showered with rays of hope as Buddha said, " all that we are, is the result of what we have thought. " (Smarika 2067, Teli kalyan Samaj, Nepal. Central office, Shantinagar, Kathmandu).

This organization is organizing many activities like shibir (camps) and bhandaras (collective feasts) in Janakpur on the occasion of Vivah Panchami, Barsik Samellan (Annual gathering), scholarship programmes etc are best examples of its service to society.

The past of this caste is very glorious. The great saint Sambhuk was of this caste. According to the journal published by Bihar, Orrisa society Rana Bhim Singh and Rana Samarat Singh were the rulers of there who belonged to Teli and Teliagarhi was named after them. According to famous historian Dr. R. C. Majumdar, Hemchandra Bikramaditya was the last emperor of India who defeated Mugal emperor Himaun was also Teli by caste. Famous Scientist Prof. and Dr. Meghnath Sah was also Teli who was born in the district of Bengal. He was world renowned scientist. There is a famous Teli temple in the court of Gwalior which has been mentioned by Kernel Tad. It is understood easily that this caste is very ancient and scholar also which discovered how to extract oil from vegetables. The people of this caste also claim that they are the descent of Mahatma Gandhi.

Deepak Chaudhary writes in his book about Teli in the following lines:

> "In the preparation to their population, their socio-economic position is of medium type. Rate of literacy among them is high. In the field of education, they have progressed a lot. They are very concious about education. This caste group has the tradition of using the surnames as-Shah, Shahu, Gupta and Teli; most of them use Shah as their surname. The major place of their settlement is mid-Tarai. " (Deepak Chaudhary: 2010. P. 85)

Karikh is their favourite local God. They also worship Goraiya, Hanuman, Meira Sultan and Govinda. They are major caste of the Vaishya group. They have different groups and sub-groups such as Kanaujia, Magahia, Mayuriya, Jounpuriya, Aurhiya, Chhapariya, Umarteli and Umarvaishya. It is generally believed that Kanayjiya had come from Kanauj, U.P.

State, Magahiya/Magadhiya from Magadh, Bihar, Chhapariya from also Bihar, India. Now a days they can inter -marriage among these groups. But they can not marry in the same gotra according to tradition.

According to the census of 2011 their total population is 369,688.

Tharus

Many scholars are of this view that Tharu people are the aborigins of the region and they are the first people to inhabit the Terai. Their settlements are called Tharuhat which is in tropical malarial areas. This is their traditional territory which is the southern-forested region of the Siwalik Hills and the southern parts of the Terai bordering India. Tharus are also found in Indian states of Bihar and U.P.

According to some scholars they are the migrants from the Thar desert of Rajasthan, India. They are said to be the descendants of the Rajput women who fled with their domestic servants because of the Muslim invasion. They did not like to be the victim of their enemies.

There is also another theory that they are not immigrants. If they were immigrant people then they have not settled in the Malaria-infected areas nearby the dense forests. They might have chosen to settle in easily accessible areas where everything was available. During the 19th and 20th centuries, some immigrants moved to the Terai from heavily and densely populated areas across the Indian border. But it was not until the 1960, when the government of Nepal sprayed DDT to control the Malaria-transmitting mosquitoes, the large numbers of hill people, or Pahari, moved into the Terai and cleared the hardwood Sal forests for cultivation.

Some scholars have thrown light on the historical background and origin of Tharu:

> "Regarding the origin of the Tharu tribe, even today, scholars have not been able to a definite and clear conclusion while some claim them to be migrants from the Thar desert in Rajasthan, India, others

> say that these are descendants of the children that were born out of the liaisons between the Rajput women and their servants who fled the Muslman invaders and after living without their spouses in these area for long periods, they ultimately cohabited with their servants thus giving birth to the breed known as the Tharu. Some Tharu state that Tharu women push the plate of food with their feet across to their husbands even today, which shows that these women still consider themselves to possess the Rajput blood, hence higher in status to their husbands. Also, that the Tharu are a mixed tribe whose ancestors had migrated into the area , seems relevant to the Rajput women and servants migration aspect." (Rajesh Gautam/ Asoke K. Thapa: 1977. P. 325).

"The Tharu economy is based on farm, and fishing, supplemented with wild grassland and forest products. Grasses are used for walls, ceilings, baskets, mats, fans and beds. In florescences for the wicks of ceremonial lamps come from one type of grass, rope is fashioned from another, and lamp stands for the Diwali Hindu festival comes from the stems of yet another. For centuries, Tharu villagers harvested grasses from the plants at the end of the monsoon and set fire to the remaining stubble."

Madhesh is mainly and culturally diverse in so many ways. It is pity to say that Tharus are not Madheshi. They are born in Madhesh and their settlement is called Tharuhat. It is also correct to say that they are the first inhabitants of Madhesh. First of all they settled in Madhesh after clearing the nearby forest. I would like to quote to support my statement:

> "Some of theTerai is culturally diverse as well. The indigenous people of the region are known as Tharu. Actually, there are many Tharu cultures, each with its own language and custom. Until recently (when Tharus began to work together to fight poverty, discrimination, and violence), members of these groups did not intermarry, understand each other, or consider themselves to belong to the same ethnic group. But inspite of this diversity, all Tharus share a history of living in the Terai. Partly because they have some genetic resistance to Malaria (though they are not completely untouched by this debilitating disease, the Tharu historically inhabitated the lowlands that outsiders considered a mysterious, dangerous, and disease ridden jungle."

The Tharus are called the people of the frontier. They have had subordinate role to play in the past but now they have pivotal role to play in politics. They have been categorised as indigenous people. Now Raj Kumar Lekhi is the chairman of Indigenous people Academy. There were several ministers of this community such as Fate Singh Tharu, Parsu Narayan Chaudhary and Labru Rana Tharu. Now Tharus are in position to influence the politics of Nepal.

I would like to quote:

> "The Terai, the area of lowest attitude in Nepal, is the home of a large ethnic group called the Tharu, who may be considered indigenous in the sense that they were probably among the earliest groups living within the territory of Nepal. Tharuwan or Tharuot, as their land is called. Also includes parts of the Churia Hills. The Tharu are especially numerous in the central areas of Chitwan, Dang, the Dhangadhi area, and further west. Their physical characteristics link them to indigenous populations of India and to other Terai groups but also to Himalayan groups." (Hannelore Gabriel:The Jewelry of Nepal. P. 165.)

Deepak Chaudhary writes in his book about Tharu in the following lines:

> "The Tharus form the largest Janjati group in population in the Tarai region of Nepal. The settlement of the Tharu inhabitants of Nepal extends from Jhapa in the east to Kanchanpur district in the west and upto the Surkhet valley. They are living in northern part of Nepal's Tarai and even upto the Siwalik range. It is essential to know the Tharus of different regions for the real study of the Tharus and their sub-groups because this group as a community contains many other sub-groups." (Deepak Chaudhary: 2012. P. 206).

Gunratne (2006) The original place of the Tharu people is unknown. No evidence has yet been found but it's taken for sure that all of the Tharus belong to the same ancestor. Several people came in Tarai from centuries and the Tharu community emerged.

The Tharus in India

"The Tharus are an example of a community which in the course of fifty-sixty years, has completely forgotten its tribal culture and is now looked upon as consisting of backward Hindus. In the census of 1941, they numbered nearly 38, 000 and were classified as a scheduled Tribe, but since they do not like being known as a tribe, they are not now included in the list. In 1948 they were recognised as caste Hindus by an order of the Nepal government. They live in the sub- mountain Tarai, in the northern part of the Champaran district. The Tharus claim that their original home was in the Thar district of Rajputana, hence they were driven by Muslim in roads. Women are considered among them as being higher in status than the men and they do not allow their husbands, or any male, to come to the kitchen, nor will they eat any food of which their husbands or sons have already partaken, customs which go against the fundamentals of Hindu family life. Tharu women are comely in appearance and have fair complexion.

Deepak Chaudhary has the same and similar view about the Tharu community of India in the following lines:

> "To quote the Census of India, 2001, the Tharu population is 85,665 in Uttaranchal. The Tharus have been settling in Dehradun, Pithauragadh, Chamauli and Udhamsingh districts. Tharu there in India is listed under the scheduled tribes. In Uttar Pradesh alone, there are some Rana Tharus living there, with the population of 83,544. They have been residing in Kheri, Balrampur and Baharaiech there in Uttar Pradesh. Kathariya and Desauria Tharus are also living there. A large number of Tharu populations live in Champaran in the Bihar state of India also. The Tharus of India are entertaining comparatively a better educational and economic condition. Government of India has been providing facilities on education and employment. " (Deepak Chaudhary: 2010 P. 210)

"As a result of the Pahari influx and deteriorating land situation, however Tharu emigration from Dang increased dramatically in the 1960s reaching its highest levels between the late 1960s and early 1970s. The movement of the Tharu households out of Dang was a very pronounced feature of the social landscape in the 1970s as is evidenced by the refrain from one of the songs published in Gotchali- 'e mora gotchali jin karo cara', means- oh my friends, do not leave Dang'. (Macconagha; Nationalist and Ethnicity in Hindu Kingdom, 1990.)

This type of notion is still prevalent in the Tharu community of Western Nepal who wear the ghunghat (veil) shawl trim, necklaces piled on top of each other, large earrings, and blouses studded with silver coins. They consider superior themselves to their husbands even now. They were mostly Hindus in earlier days but now some of them follow Buddhism also. They worship Kali, Shiva, and Mahabir and Buddha and celebrate Hindu fairs and festivals as well as Buddhism. According to one scholar:

> "They imitate Hindus in all religious ceremonials and look upon themselves as belonging to a superior caste. They are an instance of a tribe being fully converted into a Hindu caste within living memory. "

Yet anothr theory suggests that after attaining Nirvana Buddha became famous and Buddhism florished. Two schools were established. They are Mahasagahik and Sthvir. I would like to quote:

> 'Another theory for the Tharu's origins suggests that after Buddha attained Nirvana and Buddhism florished, the Mahasagahik and Sthvir schools were established. The Kapilvastu's Shakyas inclined toward Sthvir and were known as Sthirvadi or Sthvir. Later this was corrupted into Tharu.' (Dor Bahadur Bist:Tharu: P. 9-10).

I would like to quote here Ruhi Tewari's view about Tharu:

> "The Tharus are the biggest Terai Janjati group. They are spread across the Terai, with larger concentrations in some far western and eastern Terai districts." (Ruhi Tewari:The Landscape of Madhesh: P. 10)

An eminent sociologist has this following opinion about Tharu. I would like to quote here:

> "It is possible that Rajaputramani (wives of Rajput), who came from Thar (near Rajasthan, India) and the hybrids between the locals of the region might also belong to Tharu Society." (Janak Lal Sharma:1981.)

Alberuni, a Muslim historian, in eleventh century A. D. , has mentioned about the Tilawat region where the inhabitants with black complexion and flat nose called Taru used to live.

Similarly, Lama Taranath, a Tibetan saint and historian, has mentioned about Tharu Brigyud (Country of Tharus) who lived in Champaran, Wikipedia.

I would like to quote here:

> "Tharus are very thoughtful caste. Now they are well educated and settle in the villages where rest of the people live. They have their own identity and can be easily distinguished from the rest of the people. They have their own identity and can be easily distiguished from the rest of the people. Now they have their own language and culture. They are called'broken tribes' by some anthropologists which is not correct in today's context. They are scattered from the east to the west (from Mechi to Mahakali). Now they are very active in politics and are holding posts of profit even in government as well as in private sector. " (Ram Dayal Rakesh: 2005. P. 38).

> "Tharus are one of the most fascinating communities I have ever come across at the foothills of the Himalayas. Tharu community is rich in culture, tradition, dance and songs. But unfortunately, the Government. has not paid adequate attention to promote this community and its culture. (Ruger Gerend: Berlin 2011).

They speak, nowadays, their own language Tharu written in Deonagari script. But before that they used to speak different languages of Terai/Madhesh such as Hindi, Maithili, Bhojpuri and Awadhi according to their residence. R. Gautam and Asoke Thapa have very rightly remarked in the following lines. I would like to quote here:

> "While the Saptari Tharu are heard speaking with a great mixture of Maithili language which is commonly used in that region, the Tharu of Bara use a language mixed with the locally spoken Bhojpuri and the Tharu of the west, namely Banke, Bardiya, Kailali and Kanchanpur speak a mixture of Awadhi. The Dang Tharu speak a language consisting of approximately 40% Nepali, 40% Hindi and the remaining 20% consists of Maithili, Bhojpuri, Awadhi, etc.

> Deokhuri Tharu speak more of the Hindi than the other languages and thus their speech is more Hindi than anything else. Among the Tharu of Dang can be found the use of certain ancient words which have almost become extinct in the Nepali language. " (Rajesh Gautam/ Asoke Thapa Magar: 1994 P. 328).

Marriage custom in the Tharu community

Marriage custom in the Tharu community is mostly monogamous and it is also patrilocal. There is unusual and unique marriage custom in this community that is sometimes older brides are chosen for the younger grooms. This is slightly different from other castes of Tarai/Madhesh. There is no doubt that sometimes unequal marriage is also done in other castes but it is not mandatory. The Tharus also practice service, the system in which an aspiring groom is supposed to serve for the certain period to marry the girl whom he chooses to marry. Many types of marriage are prevalent in the Tharu community such as arranged marriage, elopement, marriage by capture, avid exchange marriage. Divorce is allowed. Remarriage is also in vouge.

They have aesthetic sense to a great extent. They love colourful clothing especially Tharu women like to wear beautiful and bright clothes. There is a Hindi film named Ram and Shyam in which Tharu young girls wearing gorgeous dress sing and dance which has lasting impression on the audience. They are also fond of tantalizing tattoo. The Tharu sense of aesthetics extends to the body, especially to the skin. They prefer to beautify their body with tattoo. The Tharu brides love to have tattoo on their lovely legs and enchanting arms on the auspicious occasion of marriage. This is the symbol of protection as well as purity. Their skirts are embroidered with mirror and peacock which are very shining and eye catching.

They have unflinching faith in the Hindu pantheon. They worship Hindu Gods and Goddesses but now some of them also worship Lord Buddha. Ramanand Singh former Attorney General made a statue of Buddha in his village because he was of this view that Tharus are descents of Buddha's dynasty. The Tharu women of the Dang valley decorate their walls of houses with pretty paintings of religious images of Hindu Gods and Goddesses. This is proof enough that they are religious minded as well as followers of Hindu religion.

Their houses are small but neat and clean. They prefer to live in clustered villages. They use wood and bamboo with mud as construction materials for their houses. They have generally thatched houses. A few of them have pucca buildings also to live in. Only wealthy people can afford for it. The Tharu people of the Dang valley usually live in long houses in which at least seventy to seventy five people can live together. Their main profession is agriculture and animal husbandry. They cultivate rice, maize, wheat, potatos, mustard, lentils, green vegetables and fruits. Cows and she buffalows provide milk. They drink and make curd out of it. They also prepare ghee and butter and cheese. Their is a popular saying that the Tharu people are the most egalitarian groups among the Nepalese people. The women consider themselves superior to men in this part of the land.

The Tharu people of the Chitwan valley share agricultural work and household together. They have mostly joint family. The head of the family generally make final decision in any disputes. Parents have generally no choice as to the sex of a child.

The Tharu women are fond of ornaments made of silver. They use ornaments made of gold also. One scholar has described it in the following lines:

> "Most Tharu jewelry forms can be easily linked to the Indian tradition. and many of the designs can be found south of the border in India or to the west:."

The Tharu women hanker after necklaces. They are very significant ornament for them. One scholar has this opinion about necklace:

All Tharu necklaces are usually significant. They are often large and heavy, and the Tharu wear them in multiples.

Village Gods and Goddesses of Tharu people

According to one scholar:

> "The Kuldevta, the ancestral deities, are worshipped at a shrine in the house, and are offered occasional animal sacrifices. In village

> shrines, supernatural beings, both beneficient deities and evil spirits, may be represented as rounded rocks or as balls of earth, sometimes mixed with cotton and sugar and topped by a small piece of gold and a trident. With increasing contact with their Hindu neighbours, the Tharu have also in corporated Hindu deities into their all-encompassing pantheon. Crude carvings of these sometimes are placed near village shrines."

Marriages among the Tharu community are mostly monogamous and patrilocal. An unusual feature of Tharu culture is that sometimes older brides are found for the younger men, an age difference of ten years is common. This custom, shared by other Tarai people, can effectively works as a population control device. The Tharu practice bride service, the system in which a young man has to work for the bride's parents for two or three years to 'earn'his wife before he can marry her. The Tharu can choose from several forms of marriage: arranged marriage, elopment, marriage by capture, avid exchange marriage. In an exchange marriage, a household offers one of its daughters to the household from which it has received a bride, No stigma is attached to divorce, and some Tharu divorce frequently until they have found the right partner. Remarriage after widowhood is considered desirable.

According to one scholar the Tharu community, now a days does not follow their traditions in totality. I would like to quote here:

> "If we accept the village Tharu Guruwa's perspective, the Tharu religion is a fading tradition and ritual exercise is a vanishing habit. Butwal's Tharu Guruwa laments the decline of religion as the loosening of Tharu cultural identity." (Mary Ann Maslak:Daughter of the Tharu: P. 161.)

According to the population survey of 2011 their total population is 1,737,470.

Fairs and Festivals of Terai/Madhesh

Jurshital (Baisakh April), Chaurchan (Shrawan July) for worshipping moon, Nagpanchami (Shrawan, July) to worship snakes, Rakhibandhan or Rakhi (Shrawan july) symbol of brother sister love. Krishna Asthmi (Bhadra August) to worship Lord Krishna) Indra Pooja (Anant Chaturdashi) to worship rain God.

Dashmi (Aswin Sept/Oct) to worship Goddess Durga. Lakshmi Puja (Kartik Oct.) to worship Lakshmi, Chhath (Kartik Oct) to worship sun, Bibah Panchami (Agrahan/ Nov. Dec.) to celebrate marriage of Rama Sita, Tila-Sankranti (Magh (Jan. Feb.) after bathing people take sweets. Mahashivaratri or Shivaratri (Falgun/Feb, March) to worship Lord Shiva, Hori (Fagua or Fagu) to celebrate Colours, Ram Navami (Chaitra (Mar/April) to worship Lord Ram, Shama-chakewa (Kartik) love between brother -sister, Savane Ghari (Shrawan) pooja of family God , Jitiya (Bhadra/Aswin).

Food

Food is life. Food is culture. It provides identity and incarning. It is a medium of relatedness, invested with cultural values. Understanding human food system is essential to understanding both physical survival and cultural survival. (Prof. Dr. Steventa: M. Parish)

Jurshital. main food, rice, pulse, vegetables, curd, Taruwa (veg. fry).

Jitiya: Curd, beaten rice, Banana,

Chhatha: Thekuwa, Bhusba, Kasar etc.

Holi: Meat, Malpua, Roti Veg.

Dipawali: Rice, Pulau, Curd, Taruwa of different vegs.

Traditional Sources of entertainment:

Nach: Rani Saranga, Dinabhadri Salhesh, Brijbhan. Jhijhiya, Jat- jatin. Krishnalila, Ramlila, Kirtan.

The Month of Shrawan in Maithili Culture.

The month of Shrawan is considered very sweet and soothing in Maithili culture. It is also considered very religious. This month is also very momentous in terms of season. Poets are very fond of this month. Even the great poet Kalidas has described its importance in his famous epic named Meghdoot. He has described its natural as well as material beauty and importance. His hero Yakshchha sends message to his forlorn heroine through clouds. His heroine is weeping bitterly in absence of her lover. It is in the month of Shrawan when there is soft shower of rain through out whole night. The lightening is shinning all around. The black clouds are roaming and roaring day and night. The whole sky is covered with silky and silvery clouds. It increases the pangs of separation to a great extent. Everything is stimulating and exciting. Her pain of separation has been doubled in this month because her lover is far away from her. Thus this month is not so welcoming for forlorn females. There has been a long poetic tradition of this month in Sanskrit, Hindi and Nepali languages. Kalidas's epic has become immortal in the true sense of the term. He consoles his bereaved lover by the blessings of this month. This month has been mentioned even in the folklores of Mithila. Maithili folksongs have been sweetened by the fragrance and flavour of this pleasing and pleasant month. Those folk songs which are sung in this month are called Barahmasa and Chhaumasa. These songs are sung during the whole night by men and women of Mithila. They forget the fatigue of physical labour done while planting the saplings of paddy in their fields during this month. The whole atmosphere is started resounding with these melodious folksons. Actually speaking this month is very sweet and soothing. The women folk of Mithila begin swinging in the orchards of Mango singing these sweet songs. I would like to quote one folksong in this context:

> "Sakhi (friend) peacock began to dance.
> The clouds are pouring and roaring alaround.
> The lightning is frightening me by shinning
> I feel thurst for sexual pleasure
> The night is dark and clouds are black
> Madan (the god of love) is giving pain."
> (The translation is mine)

The Maithili womenfolk love to have green Saris and bangles in this month of Madan. They also worship Lord Shiva, the enemy of Madan (Kamdeva). They also have (Mehandi) henna on their hands and feet to beautify themselves. They offer trifoliate leaves of the Bel fruit which are naturally ever green to pacify angry God Shiva. They also observe fast on every Monday of this month to please their favourite God Lord Shiva. The Terai plain is very hot and humid during the rainy season. So they wear green Saris and bangles to avoid the hot temperature and also to please Lord Shiva. The whole Terai belt looks like green velvet because of green paddy plants in the fields. They also have aesthetic sense as well as colour psychology. Green colour is considered very soothing especially in this month.

In Hinduism Shrawan is considered very auspicious month because it has religious significance. This is the fourth month according to Hindu calendar. The worshipping of Lord Shiva begings with the first Monday of this month because Monday is favourite day of Lord Shiva. It is regarded as auspicious day for worshipping and at the same time pleasing Him. So the woman folk worship Him very attentively and regularly for the long life of their husbands. The maiden girls worship Him for getting suitable husbands. It is also said that Parvati worshipped Him to get Him as her constant consort. Hindus of the world regard this month as the holiest. They throng to Shiva temples on every Monday of this month. They frequently visit Baidyanath Dham and Pashupatinath temples during this month. Some devout devotees crawl throughout the whole way to have His Darshan. Many fairs and festivals are held in this month. Nagpanchami (worshipping of Snake) is very useful festival. By offering milk and Lava (fried paddy) to the Snake God is to getrid of snake biting the whole year especially during the rainy season. Snakes frequently come out in this season and bite the people. So the people of Mithila worship the snake god every year on the fifth bright lunar day of fortnight. Rakhi (Rakshabandhan). is celebrated on the auspicious occasion of the full moon day every year. Brahmins use to wear new sacred threads on this occasion.

Sawaneghadi is also observed in the whole Mithilanchal in which family deity is worshipped by every family according to one's religion. Madhushrawani festival is also celebrated in this month with gusto. Recently married boys and girls observe this festival and pray to God Shiva for their successful conjugal life. I would like to quote here:

Religion is each individual's sacred relation with his God. This divine transformation is the result of faith in God who is Truth, Justice and Love. This is universal and common to all religions.

Dress and Ornaments

Clothes

Religion and language.

Death rites:

Death pollution.

Socio-Economic condition:

Surnames

Educational Status.

Livestock;

Health Status

Sanitation.

Drinking water.

Social status.

Eating Habits.

Social maladies (women and child marriage).

Jewellery of Tarai/Madhesh

"It was probably with the establishment of a settled agrarian society that jewellery as a from of saving and a symbol of status began to develop. The variety of design in folk jewellery evolved over the years, and the important position of the jeweller in village society also points to the fact that Jewellery was considered as the only form of investment which could be used during an emergency. Even the Vedic society, Jewellery was counted as a woman's wealth, streedhan, and comprised a part of her inheritance from her father, as well as a gift from her husband. " (Jasleen Dhamija: Indian Folk Arts and Crafts. 1977. P. 55.)

Jewellery made of gold is mostly prefered by the women of Tarai-Madhesh but they do not prefer goldplated jewellery in the true sense of the term. It not get damaged if good care is taken of it. It does not cause skin allergies. Real gold jewellery has its own historical. religious and economic importance. It is also of practical usage and aesthetics. In Hindu culture gold jewellery is closely associated with several auspicious occasions like birth and marriage. Nowadays it has become customary for rich people to use it for gifts. People who can afford, they give gold in donation. It has become indicator of social status. When it is mixed with water it serves as purifying agent and called sunpani. Gold is itself symbol of prosperity and purity. Jewellery made of gold can be preserved as family heirlooms and historical artifacts. It is also a valuable asset that serves as last resort for unseen rainy days. Wearing jewellery as fashion artifacts is very ancient concept that has been handed down from other countries and communities. It has been in fashion since times immemorial. It is in vouge in many asian countries. Pakistani women are especially very fond of gold.

It means that it is human's natural desire to decorate himsel from the very beginning. It is used to decorate with fresh flowers, wild berries, leaves and feathers and different types of tatoos on the different parts of body. It is also human's natural desire to look beautiful by decorating himself especially womenfolk. I would like to quote here again:

> "No married woman was expected to be seen without jewellery. A necklace around her neck, earrings, head ornaments and bangles are essential for every married women. It was only if she became a widow that she was denuded of Jewellery. " (Jasleeen Dhamija: 1977. P. 55).

Women of Tarai/ Madhesh are fond of jewellery whether rich or poor alike. They prefer to have pure gold jewellery either 24 carrat or 22 carrat. Even people of low profile prefer ornaments made of gold though gold is very expensive. It is considered symbol of social status. It is also very prestigious in the eyes of people. They use less silver ornaments than gold. Poor people use ornaments made of silver because they can not afford gold ornaments. They also do not use gold ornaments in feet such as Payal made of gold. It is not considered auspicious to use gold ornaments in feet. So they use gold ornaments in nose, forehead, neck and ear and finger. Men of Madhesh wear gold ornaments in fingers and arms. Ornaments used in fingers are called rings and used in arms called Annat or Bahudand. These are generally made of gold and worn by men and women equally. Now a days rich people wear bracelets made of gold on their wrists. They also use bands and belts made of gold for their watches.

I am giving a short list of jewellery of Tarai/Madhesh.

Necklace, Champakali, gold, consisting of forty two small pendants and one large one, strung on red silk covered with gold wire.

Women of Tarai/Madhesh wear necklace especially on the auspicious occasion of marriage. It is very popular among the women. It is of many colours and designs. It is made of pure gold and very popular not only in Tarai/Madhesh but in India also. It is getting popular day by day. It is also called Har in Hindi. Naulakha har was supposed to be worn by queens and princesses in ancient times. It is also the symbol of womanhood. Necklace of red colour is the most popular and it is worn by those women whose husbands are alive. It is also given to bride by groom on the occasion of wedding ceremony. It is called Tilhari in Nepali. Its colour signifies sexuality and fertility in marriage. It is understood that groom transfers life giving-force to the bride. Red colour-made necklace is especially meant for wedding purpose and on other occasions necklace made of any colour is accepted. Widows of high caste Hindus are not allowed to wear necklaces. About necklace it has been mentioned:

> "A necklace excavated at U. which is made up of finely designed pendants of lion-heads with granulated work, and supposed to have belonged to Queen Bathsheba, has a remarkable likeness to the garuda necklace prepared in Kerala. The design and the

technique are remarkably similar. " (Jasleen Dhamija: 1977. P. 55-56.)

It is also very popular in the Tharu community of Tarai/ Madhesh. I would like to quote here:

> "All Tharu necklaces are usually significant. They are often large and heavy, and the Tharu women wear them in multiples."

Ornaments worn on the forehead or suspended from the head Tilak.

This is more properly the sectarian mark, or an ornament which takes its place. Tika, Tiki, Tilki, Tikali. All these words mean special mark on other parts of the body. The Tika is also a badge of sovereignty amongst Hindus, and the application of it upon the forehead of a new ruler is one of the principal acts at an installation or coronation.

The main characters of Tharu jewellery and that of other Terai groups are that it is made of silver or silver subsitutes and that it is worn in great quantity. As well, more than other ethnic groups in Nepal the Tharu still use silver coins, both in jewelry and as copious decorations of garments including men's vest. The love of the Tharu for colourful decoration also surfaces in their use of pom-poms made of colourful yarn. They can be worn as earrings, sometimes with multiple chains emerging from them, or attached to other jewelry pieces. Still, the masters of jewelry worn by the Tharu today are only a faint echo of what was worn in the past.

Bangles

Bangles are very beautiful to look at. Red bangles are symbol of womanhood. They are considered taboos for widow women. They are also called Balas. They are made of silver and gold both. Green bangles are worn by married women on the auspicious occasion of Teej. They are also worn in the month of Shrawan which is considered very pious.

Bindi

"The bindi on the forehead is an ancient tradition in Hinduism and has religious significance. It is also sometimes referred to as the third eye and the flame, and it is an auspicious religious and spiritual symbol. "(Rajan Zed, leader of the Universal Society of Hinduism. 2013)

> " While some international blogs are calling it'a tribal finery, ' we can spot a good bindi' when we see it. " (Kritika Kapoor: The Times 2013).

" It is not meant to be thrown around loosely for seductive effects or as a fashion accessory aiming at mercantile greed. "

It means that bindi is very ritualistic, vibrant and religious decoration for the Hindu women. All dancers of Kathak, Bharat Natyam and Kuchipudi use bindi on their foreheads to attract the audience. It is also crystal clear that the bindi was an essential element of an Indian woman's cosmetic wear. In the mid-90s, it went international when singers like Gwen Stefani and Madonna started sporting it with dresses and jeans in music-videos and on the red carpet somewhere, down the line, the bindi became a forgotten traditional relic.

Kashin Fernandes writes about the bindi in the following lines:

> "The festive season in the perfect-time to flaunt this trend-on- the comeback. Use a fine-tipped eyeliner stick to make a straight vertical line, an oval, a triangle or a miniature design for a metalic look, dust a readymade sticker bindi with gold or silver powder, beads or glittering rhinestones. "

Thus the bindi is crossing its cultural border and entering in an international arena. It is also becoming an issue of hot debate and controversy at the same time. It is very popular in rural area: I would like to quote:

> "The use of bindi is common amongst the tribals. This is a head ornament similar to the shingarpatta having a central pendant which hangs from the parting of the hair on to the forehead, and from which intricately worked chains with silver globules extend on both sides upto the ear, thus framing the face of the wearer. The

> bindi ends with the karanphool Jumka, which is suspended from the ear-lobes. "

Jhumka

It is very commonly used by the women folk of Tarai-Madhesh and North Bihar. It is made of silver and gold and worn in ears. There are many petals in it. Its sound is very sweet and at the same time very sexy. It excites people and also attracts them. There is a very famous Hindi film song which goes like this:

"Jhumka gira re Bareli ke bazar me."

Now a days people call it earrings but in ancient times womenfolk were fond of silvermade Jhumkas. I would like to quote here:

> " Till almost the early part of the 20th. century, both men and women wore silver ornaments. This tradition is less visible for men though it still survives in rural area. Since silver was considerably cheaper, jewellery made from silver was often heavier. Silver ornaments traditionally worn include the Jhumakas (earrings), the Chandrahar and Hansali (necklace), cummerbunds (waist band), Tika (forehead ornament) and the Payal (anklet). Silver jewellery particularly coin necklaces are still extremely popular with women in the hills. " This is also called Karanful: a star-shaped earring which is fully described in which a full account of Jhumka.

Hasuli

It is generally made by silver but rich people use Hasuli made of gold. It is very traditional ornament, women wearing it from time immemorial. It is also called Hasli in some parts of India and Nepal -Terai. Now it is generally made of gold only. It has been said about Hasali:

> "The hasuli was also generally worn by the lower caste groups. The Chandrahaar, worn below the hasuli, was also patronised by the same group. The hasali, common all over India, is made in a number of designs. " (Jaslin Dhamija: 1977. P. 58)

Hasuli, a thick and collar-like ornament is traditional designs worn by women even today. Easily the most stunning neck ornament is the Chandrahar which is a bunch of long silver chains linked by engraved or enamelled silver plaques. There also exists a strong tradition of wearing heavy anklets, bangles and silver bracelets with clasps in the shape of crocodile or lions heads. There is a superstition in the Madhesh society that gold made ornaments should not be worn in feet. So the silvermade payal and and the toe—ring were popular across all classes. Toe-rings is also called Bichhiya in Madheshi society. It is considered an important symbol of marital status. The Payal has a long Hindu tradition and is still considered a valuable gift for new-born baby girls. Womenfolk of Terai-Madhesh use it in their daily life. It beautifies their feet to a great extent. Another type of Payal is called Paijeb. It is bigger and also heavier than Payal. Payal and Paijeb are often studded with semi precious stones. Silver commerbunds and keyrings are the symbols of married life of womanfolk of Madhesh. Now silver jewellery is reviving because they like to have it. Indians and foreighners are fond of it. They use it like antiques. I would like to quote here:

"The silver jewellery is now more popular than ever as the preferred choice for the educated elite. It is more affordable and has more contemporary designs available than gold. Today numerous silversmiths cater to the Indian market with purely contemporary and traditional designs. The women today are content with silver necklaces. "

> "This round collar is worn tight around the neck or resting on their collar bones. "

Most of the ornaments of Tarai/Madhesh can easily be compared to the Indian tradition, and many of the designs can be available in south of the border in India . The main attributes of Tarai/Madhesh jewellery is made of silver or silver substitutes. It is worn in great quantity by women of Tarai/Madhesh.

Chudamani

Chudamani is very ancient jewellery of Tarai- Madhesh. It is worn at the parting of the hair by women folk. It is made of gold and silver both. It has been mentioned in the Ramayan written by Tulasi Das that Sita used to wear it and she handed over it to Hanuman when he went to find out her in Lanka as a symbol for Rama. I would like to quote here the very line:

"Chudamani utar tab dinha".

Its very shape is like lotus flower with many petals. I would like to quote here:

> "The Chudamani, shaped like a full-blown lotus with many petals, was worn at the parting of the hair and is similar to the present-day bore of Rajasthan. In the Ramayan, there is mention of Sita wearing a nishika necklace. Nishika, a gold coin, is also referred to in the Jataka stories. It is obvious that even in those days wearing of necklaces made up construction. It is pendant suspended from the pierced septum by a gold ring. It is very light in weight. So it is very easy to wear. I would like to quote:
>
> Bulaki: "By and large the bulaki for Indo-Nepalese women are small, comfortable gold rings, often flattened. "

Nath

Nath is also a nose ornament very much like Bulaki, but it is bigger than bulaki. It is the symbol of chastity, purity and also virginity. To break nath means to impure a woman. This clause is very common among prostitutes. It is very popular among Madheshi especially in the North Indian culture. It is also worn by the Muslim community womenfolk. It is also constructed according to the Indian ornament style. For this purpose women pierce their nose which is painful sometimes. They want to adore themselves on the occasion of marriage.

I would like to quote here about nose ornament:

> "The nose ornament is worn all over India. It has variations from the simple Lawang, clove, Phuli, the elaborately worked stud, or nath, the nose-ring worn in the right nostril, and the bulli, the nose-ring worn in the centre just over the lips.' (Jasleen Dhamija: 1977. P. 57.)

Earrings

Earrings ornament is worn in ears, so it is called earrings. The Tarai/Madhesh women pierce the lobule, concha, helix, and even the tragus of the ear to show an array of modest to extragant ear-adornment. it is worn by married and unmarried women. It is very popular in India and Nepal. I would like to quote here:

> "For Indo- Nepalese in most areas, rather insignificant variations of hoop earrings suffice for ear adornment, these are rarely ornate, and often merely plain wire. "

Godana (Tatoos)

Godana is also an ornament but it is quite different from other ornaments. It is also an adoration and ornamentation of body of woman folk of Tarai/Madhesh. It is engraved in several parts of body with the help of needle. It was very painful in the early times but now a days it is not so painful because it is done by machine. It was very popular in ancient times but it is not so popular because of fear of infection and also fear of Aids disease. In rural areas of Tarai- Madhesh the Natin women use the same needles for many women. Nat and Natin are wanderer castes and they roam from one house to another for this purpose for the support of their livelihood. Now a days this profession is in danger because of its modernisation but this body art is original and ancient. There is a folksong which describes the very old profession of Nat- Natin. I would like to quote here some of the lines of this folk art:

> The womanfolk are fond of embroidering and beautifing of their several parts of their body such as hands, legs, chests, palms, torsos, necks and arms with godana. It was a permanent beautiful art of body which once engraved continue lifelong. This is a folk art very popular once upon a time in Terai/Madhesh. Now it has become body art but it is disappearing slowly from there due to modernisation and urbanisation. The womanfolk are not coping with this at all. Now this has become a craze among youngsters of western countries. The Nepali youths are following it blindly forgetting its cultural charm because there is a description of various Gods and Goddesses in it. They use to reflect their feelings related to their respective gods and goddesses. It has sociological, cultural and religious value. There is a book named 'Bodies of Subversion:A Secret History of Women and Tatoo. It was published in 1997. Now its third edition is also available in the market. Its celebrated writer, Margot Miffin has reviewed it in the western world from a female

perspective which is very similar with the Madheshi perspective because it is very popular in the woman community. In the words of Miffin tatoos are no longer revel emblems. They are a mainstream fashion choice. They are emblems of empowerment in an era of feminist gains. They are also badges of self determination at a time when controvercies about abortion rights, date rape and sexual harassment. The writer is of view that it has' the ability to degrade as well as to enhance, to invoke the sacred and the inane'. She has very candid and vivid view of tatoos in the following lines:

> "Tattooing shifts the focus of women's issues from society to the self; that tattooed women are empowered only in their minds. "

There is an interesting account of Tattooing in the western world. The writer has focussed on the history of tattooing in Europe and America. According to her tattooing was an upper-class social fad in Europe in the late 19th century. The fad spread to America. According to The Newyork World's percent of American society women were tattooed. By the 1920s, tattooed women were mostly to be seen in freak shows and in circus acts, where they could make more money than tattooed men. But it is loosing its charm in the western countries also to day. According to the survey conducted by the Archives of Dermatology 69 percent of tattooed women are in favour of removing tattoos because they have become the symbols of stigma in the society.

Tilhari

Tilhari is composed of seven beads finely worked in high-carat gold, adds the beauty of newly-wed brides. It is mandatory for all brides whether rich or poor. It is given on the day of marriage to the bride by the husband after he has already placed red Pote around the neck. By wearing this the bride wishes long life of her husband. It is very popular now a days. Womanfolk of Terai-Madhesh are fond of jewellery whether rich or poor. Sometimes marriage is not materialised in want of it. They wear it on the auspicious occasion of marriage generally and in party particularly. I would like to quote here:

> "Jewellery items the bride wears, excluding the tilhari, are of secondary importance to this item. Its colour signifies sexuality and fertility in marriage, that is, lineage continuity, and it is through

> the consummation of the marriage that the husband transfers the life giving-force, symbolized by the red of the Saubhagya items, to the bride. "

Muslims of Terai/Madhesh

"Do not conceal from
Allah whatever is in your breasts hoping it may be hidden.
Allah knows whatever is concealed.
There is no God but Allah. "
(David Waines. 2005)

"South Asia is not a mere frontier of Islam , but an integral part of the Islamic world, making a distinctive contribution to the life of the whole. For many centuries it has been interacting with Hinduism by way of both attraction and repulsion, but it has not severed its links with the heartlands of Islam. More recently Indian Islam preceded the heartlands in receiving and responding to the European impact." (Aziz Ahmed, An Intellectual History of Islam in India, 1969).

Islam has been living tradition in South Asia from last so many centuries.

Islam is one of the major religions of over 140 million people in India alone. According to the census of 2011 the total population of Muslims in Nepal is 1,164,255 among which 584,754 is male and 579,501 is female. Muslims are also called Musalman. There has not been sufficient literature on the Muslims of India what to talk about Nepal. One scholar has pin-pointed this lack of literature in the following lines:

> "In order to address the lack of writings on India's Muslims and their emerging identities apart from questioning analytical frameworks and epistemological assumptions, the present need is to be aware of Islam in South Asia as a living tradition, however defined, and as a dynamic force. " (Mushirul Hasan. Introduction).

However some scholars have done serious studies about Muslims and their religion Islam. In this context there are some celebrated works of scholars like Barbara D. Metcalf's 'Islamic Revivalism in British India, Rafiuddin Ahmed's The Bengal Muslims (1860-1906), Mehran Kamrava's. The New

Voices of Islam, Francis Robinson's Islamic Revival in Islam and Muslim History in South Asia and 'The Ulama of Farangi Mahall and Islamic Culture in South Asia, Devotional Islam & Politics in British India, Ahamad Riza Khan Barelwi and His Movement, Christian W. Troll, Muslim Shrines in India, Musirul Hasan (ed.), Islam, Communities and the Nation:Muslim Identities in South Asia and Beyond, Toby M. Howarth, The Twelve Shia as a Muslim Minority in India, 'Met Calf Ahmad Hossan's India's Muslims, David Waines: An Inroduction to Islam, David Gilmartin's ' Customary Law and Shariat in Punjab, Rafiuddin Ahmad's "Conflicts and Contradictions in Bengali Islam: Problems of Change and Adjustment, Anna Suvorova's 'Muslim Saints of South Asia: The Eleventh to the Fifteenth Centuries, Nile Green, Indian Sufism since the Seventeenth Century, Nationalism and Communal Politics in India, Chitralekha Zutshi's Languages of Belonging: Islam, Regional Identity and the Making of Kashmir, Mridu Rai's Hindu Rulers, Muslim Subjects:Islam, Rights, and the History of Kasmir, Barbara Daly Metcalf's Moral Conduct and Authority: The Place of Adab in South Asian Islam, Katherin P. Ewing (ed. Shariat and Ambiguity in South Asian Islam, Satish Saberwal & Mushirul Hasan (eds.) Assertive Religious Identities:India and Europe, Olivier Roy, Globalised Islam: The Search for a New Ummah, Tariq Ramadan's Western Muslims and the Future of Islam. It is a matter of great satisfaction that now many scholars are interested in the study of Muslims and their religion in details. Several anthropologists and sociologists are engaged in its research. One scholar has expressed it in very convincing way I would like to quote it here:

> "Today, more and more scientists are engaged in 'understanding' Islam and 'observing'Muslim societies within historically informed social contexts. With one- third of the world's Muslims now living as members of a minority, they are busy exploring their responses to globalisation, westernization, and the impact of living in a minority. " (Olivier Roy, Globalised Islam:The Search for a New Ummah, 2004.).

The other scholar is in favour of the detailed debate on it. I would like to quote here:

> "I started with a plea to draw Islam in South Asia into the contemporary discourses on colonial and postcolonial writings. The Cambridge historian Herbert Butterfield had reminded us long ago that we should be ourselves not quite autonomous or unconditional, but a part of the great historical process:' not pioneers merely, but also passengers in the movement of things.' (H. Butterfield, The Whig Interpretation of History 1931 P. 50.).

In this context Deepak Chaudhary writes in his book about Muslims in the following lines:

> "The followers of Islam religion are called Musalman or Muslim. In the world, the followers of Islam religion have the second largest number after the followers of Christianity. Islam, Christianity and Jewish religions are said to have originated from the regions of Arab. The devotees of these religions believe that the creator has sent different emissaries/ messengers in the world at different periods. In Islam, the first messenger is called Adam and the same Adam (pronounced Anglically) is in the Christian religion too. " (Deepak Chaudhary: 2010. P. 235). :
>
> Paigambar Mohammad is the only one God of Muslims who is the propounder of Islam. He was born in the shrine of Mecca in the state of Saudi Arabia in 570 A.D.

It is believed that Muslims first of all entered into Nepal in the thirteenth century from neighbouring country India. In the year 1334 A.D. the Muslim ruler attacked on Simraungargh and destroyed it completely. Consequently the king of Muslim identities Nation that state fled towards the foothills of the Himalaya. First of all Muslims came in Tarai to settle permanently. After that they moved towards the Kathmandu valley during the Malla period.

Anthropologist Dor Bahadur Bista writes in his book 'People of Nepal' about Muslims in the following lines:

> 'The Kashmiri or other Muslims of Kathmandu entered at the end of the fifteenth century and around the beginning of the 16th century, the period of Ratna Malla. ' (Dor Bahadur Bista: 1996. P. 181).

Their settlements are scattered from Terai/ Madhesh to the Kathmandu valley to hilly region. But they are densely inhabitated in the two districts of Nepal namely Rautahat and Banke. They win election from these two districts quite often because they get majority of votes. They are very religious minded people. They read Namaj five times a day facing towards 'Kaba or Mecca'. People above the age of 12 are supposed to read every day but on every Friday it is mandatory. It is considered sacred to read Namaj in group in mosque. There is at least one mosque in every village in Tarai-Madhesh. It is also believed that Muslims should perform Haz once at least in their lifetime. Their main motto is to go to Macca/Madina once in life on pilgrimage. They consider very pious to go on pilgrimage for getting salvation. This is compulsory for male members only.

Fairs and festivals

Religious festivities were and continue to be a delightful diversion in the general life of Nepali people. Tourists are highly impressed by its diverse beauty. They are fond of the hectic gaiety of the people at village fairs and festivals, rites and rituals of ordinary people. They also like their singing and dancing with various traditional local musical instruments.

Roza is considered most important festival which is observed fasting from sunrise to sunset. It is compulsory for adult members of the Muslim Community. It is observed strictly according to Islamic calendar every year. It is very difficult festival in terms of fasting. It has its own ethical code of conduct which is strictly followed during this period. Drinking, eating, smoking and sexual intercourse are not allowed. It is taken as religious crime. It is observed during the month of Ramajan. It falls in the ninth month of their calendar. It is observed according to the movement of the moon because it differs accordingly. It is necessary for both male and female. Only sick people and children are exempted. It is observed for whole day and in the evening special type of Namaj called 'Tarabi' is recited every day during the period. Fasting in Islam has great religious value. Fasting and maintaining cleanliness of body and surroundings is the austerity at the mental level. It is supposed to be necessary for everyone, failing which is taken as crime.

"Fasting has become synonymous to the Muslman people the world over. Their Roza has made others truly wonder about the force that drives them to such abstainence in a world wrecked with innumerable temptation. The Muslman of Nepal also are no exception. They fast throughout in holy month of Ramzan and offer Namaj five times a day, eating only after and before the sun sets and rises respectively. The month of Ramzan starts on the first day of the bright fortnight while Roza commences, as soon as the cresent moon is seen and ends with the reappearance of this cresent at the end of the month. This means the cresent goes through its sequence of waxing and waning for one full cycle. "

Roza is much more than just not fasting. It also means refraining from evils thoughts, actions and words. It also provides an opportunity to realize the pain of poor through out the world because they are deprived of food and other essential necessities of life. Millions of Muslim people visit mosque everyday especially Friday. Roza is one of the five pillars of Islam religion. The other four pillars are Shahadat (Faith), Salat (Prayer), Zakat (Charitable giving) and Hajj (the holy pilgrimage to Makkah). The month long abtenence will conclude with the celebration of Eid. ul Fitre the next month. (Rajesh Gautam and Asoke K. Thapa Magar. 1994 P. 100.).

Here I support Deepak Chaudhary's view:

> "The second category of the Muslims includes those Muslims who were converted from Hindu in the latter phase. In Madhesh, the second categories of Muslim are found in a large number. ' (Deepak Chaudhary: 2010. P. 240.).

Moharrum

This festival is observed with great pomp and show every year by the Muslims of India and Terai/ Madhesh on equal footing. Even some Hindu people also participate in this festival to show fraternity and feeling of brotherhood between Muslims and Hindus. On this occasion the sacrifice of Hassan Hussain, grandson of Mohammed is highlighted. They also sing folksongs in his honour and dance with sticks.

Special food is offered each morning during the first month for ten days in the name of Hussain. This festival is called Daha in the local languages of Terai/Madhesh. On the occasion of Moharrum one can enjoy a motley crowd of drummers, one or two village gymnasts, young wannable wrestlers, stick fighters, sword swingers and spear thrusters. Tazia, a paper temple is made on this occasion. A big fair is also held on this auspicious occasion.

I would like to quote:

> "The Muslman in the terai enact the scene of Krbla where Hussain fought to his last breath. Sticks are used instead of the swords, and these sticks are whirled along with their bodies, showing great speed, dexterity and seriousness in this stick play. Being experts there are hardly any cases of participants being hurt. Thus Muharam is concluded. " (Rajesh Gautam/Asoke K. Thapa Magar: 1994. P. 103).

Shab-I-Barat festival is celebrated by eating decent dishes on this occasion. They keep night vigil and visit the graves of dead relatives. They also pray for the welfare of both the living and the dead. It occurs on the eleventh day of Shaban, the eighth month in the Islamic lunar calendar. This festival continues for the whole day. People break it by eating enchanting eateries. They prepare descent dishes and several kinds of sweets and invite their relatives, neighbours and friends for enjoying it. They keep vigil for the whole night and pray to Allah for the well being of the living and dead of their family.

Bakra-Eid is very important festival of Muslims. It is cebrated for three consecutive days beginning on the tenth day of the 12th month. Many Muslim people sacrifice goats on this occasion. They enjoy and make merry and meet people with love and affection. They pray several times to God. On this occasion they also go to Mecca for performing Haz which is held annually.

Besides, they also assemble on every Friday to offer Namaj in mosques in a mass.

Eid: Beginning: When the Prophet of Islam sighted the new moon of Shawwal, he said: ' O God, make this month for us a month of peace. "This means that this month is meant for peaceful activities, and not only that, it is the beginning of a new peace culture that has to be continued throughout the year. Eid-ul-Fitr is one of the two major festivals of the Muslim tradition. It comes just after the end of Ramadan, that is, on Shawwal 1. Ramadan is the month of the Quran when Muslims observe fast. But according to Islamic teaching, fasting is not only for the sake of fasting. It is for the sake of spiritual detachment. Abstaining from food is only a symbol. This practice symbolises the fact that Muslims must detach themselves from other activities and concentrate on the study of the Quran. I would like to quote:

> " In fact, the practice of fasting has a greater purpose;that is, studying the Quran and finding the deeper meaning of the word of God. This practice enhances spirituality and makes the individual an intellectually developed person. In other words, the month of Ramadan is meant for the acquisition of divine wisdom from the Book of God to make one a more awakened person.

Maulana Wahiduddin Khan: Essence of Eid al-Fitr:The Republica August 10. 2013.

Eid is celebrated the day after Ramjan or Roja every year. It is also called Eid Id-ul-Fitr which is very popular among the Muslim community. Even non- Muslims also join in its jubilation whole heartedly. It is celebrated for three consecutive days making merry and merriment. Children and youths also take part in it enthusiastically. They assemble at mosques in jolly mood and offer prayers to Allah their only one God on this earth. They also express their thankfulness for the success of this favourite festival. They also give alms to the poor and needy people for their satisfaction. I would like to quote here:

> "This happiness of the Muslman people is further expressed by their activities of alms giving. This is basically a sort of annual get together of the community and performing activities such as praying for the poor and needy, and also offering to Allah for His

blessing on them. " (Rajesh Gautam and Asoke K. Thapa. Magar. 1994 P. 104-105.).

This festival is also an auspicious occasion for prayer, charity, warm and cordial family gatherings, communal harmony, merriment after dawn to dusk fasting for complete one month. It is the last month of Ramadan and the whole Muslim Community looks forward to the Eid especially for the grown ups, the month-long fasting is as revered as the day they break the fast. This is called Eid-ul- Fitr. Fitr in Arabic means charity, is another important aspect of the festival. It is mandatory for all the Muslims, especially those who are well-off, to other charity to the needy. Main motto of the Eid is to please the Allah. It is celebration on the first date of Shawl, which is the tenth month of the Islamic calendar. During this festival the Muslims exchange gifts and greetings with their neighbours as a mark of brotherhood. Eid is the most pleasant festival for children because they get delicious dishes and gifts they like.

All people go to the mosque where the Imams preach the Lord's messages. It is followed by thanksgiving prayers. Thereafter, they visit their near and dear ones and take homemade sweets like vermicelli, dates and kheer. Observing fasting without taking a drop of water from the dawn to the dusk is not only fasting but it is also controlling one's sense organs so as to abstain from wrong thoughts and deeds. The Allah commands his followers to read the holy Quran throughout the month of Ramadan and put it practice throughout the year. Roza means abstinence in Arabic. The significance of this festival is also interpreted as a good time to bring people together in harmony and gratitude. Markets are full with different dishes, apparels and other items which are liked by people. Fancy and food items mostly dominate the festival. A historian of religion says that every religion begins as a universal ideology, but eventually gets reduced to a community culture. So Eid is community culture in the true sense of the term. I would like to quote here:

"Observing Eid ul-Fitr as merely a day of eating and drinking is a diminished form of Eid ul-Fitr. It amounts to observing the form, while abandoning its true spirit. The above description of Eid is an ideal prescribed in the original texts. But in every religious community there are examples of degeneration and Muslims are not an exception."

Maulana Wahiduddin Khan. Essence of Eid-ul-Fitr. Republica. August 10. 2013.

Actually speaking Islam is a religion of peace. It spreads the message of peace through this festival of Eid. The true essence of Eid has been elaborated in the following lines:

> "Islam lays great stress on peaceful relationship among people and tries to promote the culture of peace in different ways- for example, saying 'May peace be upon you' at the time of greeting. Eid is also a part of this culture. When Muslims say two units of prayer in the morning, they say at the end, Peace be upon you. 'Thus they address the whole of humanity. After observing this practice, they go out and are required to follow this spirit in their broader interaction with others. " (Maulana Wahiduddin Khan:Essence of Eid-ul- Fitr. The Republica: 10th. August 2013.).

This way we can say that it increases brotherhood relationship among the people of the whole world. Universal brotherhood is its slogan in short.

Id-ul-Adha/ Zuha: This festival of the Muslim community falls on the 10th. day of Dul Hajjah. It is the 12th month of the Islamic calendar. Its another name is Bakrid. It is observed for three consecutive days with great pomp and show. Haj is very favourite pilgrimage of the Muslim community. After the completion of this pilgrimage people observe this festival every year. They assemble at mosques and offer prayers collectively. It includes those people also who have not completed Haj. They rejoice together.

Marriage Custom in Muslim Society

The marriage system in the Muslim society is a big auspicious occasion like the Hindu society. But it is not the same. Some different custom is performed. First of all Maiyon is performed before the marriage. It is pre-nuptial ceremony in which Mehndi (Henna) practice is performed. I would like to quote here:

> "Maiyon and Mehndi take place the Muslim society too in the name of Mehr. Mehr is promised bride price, in vague still today in the Muslim community. It is financial dealing between the two sides. It has been present from time immemorial. This is given and taken in cash and kind. I would like to quote here one scholar's opinion: Once the proposal is taken seriously and accepted, negotiations for fixing the Mehr begin- the bride's family always wanting it to be higher than the bridegroom's. Generally it is fixed in between the two positions for an amount acceptable to both the families. Comparatively, the amount of Mehr is less if the bride and bridegroom are cousions- parallel or cross, or are closely ralated. The Mehr, in case of strangers is likely to be higher, the assumption being that there is greater security and stability in marrying close relatives also, being too fussy about higher Mehr when the two parties involved are close relatives would be tantamount to casting as persons on the bridegroom's family." (B. S. Baviskar & Tulsi Patel 2010).

Mehr is meant for security, sustainability, surity, safety and stability of conjugal life of bride and bridegroom. It is necessary to some extent for the continuity of marriage in the Muslim community other wise there is very easy to break relation. This saying also ensures and increases the possibility of dowry system in the Muslim community. I would like to quote:

> " Mehr is seen as providing security to the bride and stability to the marriage and is, therefore a source of strength to the Muslim women. " (B. S. Baviskar &Tulsi Patel 2010. P. 46).

Dor Bahadur Bist writes about Muslim in the following lines:

> "In physical appearance Muslims do not look any different from other Mediterranean physical types living in Kathmandu and throughout Nepal, and they are not easily distinguishable from Brahamans, Chhetris and some Newars of Indian origin. In dress and customs, however, some Kathmandu Muslims men distinguish themselves either by growing beards or by wearing a turkish hat, or both. By far the large majority do not dress much differently from the non- Muslim Nepalis around them." (Dor Bahadur Bist: People Of Nepal: P. 177.)

Their mother tounge is Urdu which is quite closely related to Hindi but the script is quite different. But the Muslims of Terai/ Madhesh do not speak chaste Urdu. They speak languages spoken in the areas where they happen to be living. So their language is influenced by the provincial languages which are spoken in that area. One way we can say that they speak mixed language. Their culture is quite original and they are ardent lovers of their own culture. They celebrate their fairs and festivals theire own way from the time immemorial. Dor Bahadur Bist has right view about the Muslims of Terai/ Madhesh:

> "Most Terai Muslims are farmers. A very few of them are tailors and bangle-sellers. Most of them are fairly self- sufficient farmers, a very few are landless wage earning labourers and even fewer are rich. " (Dor Bahadur Bist:People of Nepal: P. 178.).

But the condition of Muslims living in Terai- Madhesh has been changed drastically. Now their financial condition is also improving satisfactorially some how or other. Now they are also very much interested in the political field from village level to central level. Some of them were elected in the constituent assembly. A few of them became ministers also. This way they are also coming to the forefront in all walks of life. Muslim women are also following the same suit. Sekha Chand Tara is the present chairperson of Nepal women's commission. Mohana Ansari is one of the commissioners. Karima Begam was the minister of state.

According to the population of 2011 census they are 1,164, 255 in number but their presence in the government machinery is very negligible. Now they have Muslim commission which is supposed to look after their allround welfare.

Some Sanskars of the Madheshi Society

Naming ceremony

After performing Chhathiyar the naming ceremony is celebrated in many castes. This ceremony is observed on the sixth day in some castes but in some castes it is observed on twelveth day. Some castes seek the advice of astrologers and wise men of the society for naming their newly born kids. They also organize small party to feed their relatives and well wishers for having the first sight of the newly born baby. They present small gifts to the baby.

Annaprasan

This ritual of feeding is celebrated after six months in some of the castes of the Madheshi community. There is no hard and fast rule for this ritual. some of the castes do not observe this. It is observed by high caste people throwing a party but it is not customary for all castes. Most of the middle class people do not observe this. Some of them while eating themselves, the newly born baby also eats with them the same food regardless of age. Hence, it is not compulsory for all to observe this. There is no fixed day for celebrating this ritual. For five and six months only liquid is provided to the newly born babies.

Muran/ Mundan

The Madheshi people perform this ritual named Mundan which means shaving of the initial hair on the boy's head. This is a short ritual which is done by barber on the auspicious occasion. They perform Pooja to their tutelary Gods wishing long life for their children. They also pray to other Gods for their safety and wellbeing. The boy is kept in his mother's lap and his hair is chopped off by a village barber for which he gets good remuneration in cash and kind. While the hair is being cut, the mother is very careful that the cut hair does not fall on the ground. She collects it in her Anchal or tip of her sari spreadout under the boy's head. The collected hair is taken and thrown into a river nearby if she can go to the river otherwise the collected hair dump into a bamboogrove. There is a general belief that boy's hair may grow like the river, long and continuous. or the hair will grow like the bamboo grove, tall and straight and thick. People even go to the place of pilgrimage like Janakpur in Nepal and Babadham in Bihar in neighbouring country India. This is concidered auspicious occasion on which a small party is thrown to the invited guests, neighbours, relatives and acquaintaces. This is an occasion of rejoicing and entertaining.

Clan

Clan is an important social institution within each caste and ethnic group. The clan group is the main basis for settling marriage and other social relation. This distinguishes people from one group to another. There are many groups and sub-groups in any community.

Kinship

Consanguine relationship is blood related kinship. In blood relation, father, mother , son, daughter, brother, sisters etc are considered close relations. Maternal uncle, wife's brother and sister and husband's or wife's parents come under the final relationship.

E.B. Tylor in Dictionary of Sociology defines kinship as "The social recognition and expression of genealogical relationship" both consanguineal and affinal. He further argues that 'kinship system may include socially recognized relationship based on supposed as well as actual genealogical ties. kinship terminology in the Madheshi community in the local languages is as follows:

Husband, wife, elder brother, uncle, aunt, elder brother's wife, elder sister's husband, elder sister, wife brother, wife's sister/ wife of younger brother/husband's elder brother (bhaisur), husband's younger brother(dewar), wife of dewar (dewarani) wife of bhaisur (jethani), husband'sister (nanad), husband's father's sister (fufu), father's sister (piusi), sister of mother (mausi), husband of mausi (mausa), mother's brother (mama), wife of mama (mami), Mother's Father (nana), Mother's Mother (nani), Father's mother (dadi) Father's father (baba), sister's son (bhanja, bhagina) sister's daughter (bhagini), husband's or wife's mother (saus), husband's or wife's father (sasur), Daughter in law (putoh), husband of daughter (jamaya or damad), father of son or daughter in-law (samadhi), Mother of son daughter-in-law (samdhini.)

Hindus and Buddhists intermarry

The caste system is the basis of the present Hindu society. The word caste was coined from the Latin word castes and was loosely used by the Portuguese to denote the purity of blood. The castes emerged after the Varna system, the four-fold division of society. A caste is almost invariably endogamous. Members of common gotra (clan) name may not marry each other. Hence they practice clan exogamy. There is no such view as Aryan invasion but they assimilate them in one thread that is Hindusim. Hinduism was prominent and prevalent during that period. Subodh K. Singh (2010) has also refuted that there was no Aryan invasion. He is of the opinion that Aryan was a mythical race. He has expressed his opinion in the following lines:-

> "The time has come to discard such mythical race, which was used as a tool by the Europeans to divide and rule the people of the Indian subcontinent. Dr. Frawley, Vamadeva Shastri at the American Institute of Vedic studies, say that the Aryan in theory is an example of European colonialism turned into a historical model.

Let us have a look on the word Arya. The word Arya or Aryan refers to one who is righteous and noble for example Arya putra, Arya kanya. It is found nowhere in the Vedic Literature & Smitris that the word Arya denotes to race or language. But this is a wrong notion. There is a mention of Aryan in the Vedic period. "It is likely that the Vedic Gods who eventually became established in India were the result of the fusion of ideas brought by the invading Aryans and those of indigenous people such as the Dravidians."

The Aryan people were very polite and kind. They were not cruel and heartless. When they entered into the territory of India they showed sympathy with the local people. One scholar has noted down this characteristics of the Aryan race in the following lines:

> "When the Aryans came to India, they came across the local inhabitants whom they called Dasas or Dasyus. Instead of killing them, as the other invaders did, they tried to absorb them by giving them a lower status in the society. With the passage of time the

> system became four classes. The social structure in ancient India was based on scientific principles. " A. G. Matchell: Hindu Gods and Goddesses: UBS publishers N. Delhi).

It was Max Mueller who introduced the word 'Arya' in 1853 into the English language referring to Aryan race and language. According to Mueller's etymological explanation 'Aryan' the word is derived from ar (to plough, to cultivate.) Four Arya Satya (Four Noble Truths). Therefore, the meaning of Arya is given as 'excellent, best, followed by respectable, and a noun, master, lord, worthy, honourable, upholder of Aryan values.

Therefore, Aryan means 'cultivator', or farmer.

There was good mingling of Aryan and Dravidian society in ancient Aryabrata. According to one Indian scholar

> Aryan society, to begin with, was one and undifferentiated. But the contacts with the Dravidians introduced Varna or colour as the first mark of obvious distinction very soon, however, that acquired a technical meaning , and became a level of social differentiation. S. R. Sharma, Ancient Indian History and Culture P. 89.

Aryan culture is an old one. It is original in nature but in course of time it has also changed a lot. So we can say that culure is dynamic and not static S.R. Sharma has righty observed the nature of change in it. "Aryan or Hindu society has certain fundamental features which have remained unchanged in the course of ages. Some of them have been derived from the Vedic traditions, while others have come in from other and later resources. The transformation from the Vedic to the Hindu society came about so imperceptibly that, at this distance, it is as difficult to distinguish between the original and the borrowed elements as it is between the Aryan and the Dravidian already mentioned.

Therefore, there are four divisions of Aryan society: Brahmins, Khastriya, Vaishyas and Sudras. They are called Chaturabarna or four Varnas, the tendency persisted and resulted in the ultimate creature of innumerable divisions but neither upon colour nor upon occupation but upon birth and the observance of food and marriage restrictions. There are countless castes. There is no exact and authentic date regarding this. According to one scholar jaisi refers more than once to the traditional list of chhatisa jatis (36 castes), including Brahmans (with sub caste Gaur), Kshatriyas (with sub castes such as Bais, chandels, Tomass, Gaharwars, Panwars, Guhilets, Bahels, pariharts, Khatis (Khatri) Kayasthas, Kalhans 'Pachmans and other vaisyas (Bania, Agrawals and so on) an also kalwars (distillars), Barias (sellers and cultivators of betel leaves), Patuis (braiders or makers of strings or tapes), and the low caste Dharas and Hadis (Called Mehtars) and Halakhors by the Moghals.

Nicolo Conti and Taver Nier, the Italian and French travellers of the 13th and 17th centuries respectively count 84 and 72 castes. But neither jaisi nor these travellers give correct figures of the different castes and professional class. Their subdivisions in Mughal times had become to numerous to mention.

One Indian scholar has highlighted the admixture of different castes in the following lines:

> The Brahmans and the Kshatryas belong to the same racial stock, but the latter are more mixed than the former. The original Kshatriyas lost their purity of blood by inter marriage with later Rajputs. The various artisan castes such as the Koiri, Kurmi, Kahar and Ahir, don't differ very much from each other in physical characteristics yet they represent a mixture of various racial strains. The Doms and Chamars are racially even farther removed from tribal groups. Leaving aside the large hybrid elements among them the average Dom is, by modern standard, a handsomer person than the Chamar. The incidence of handsome and attractive features among women is a cause rather that the consequence of miscogenations. The socalled higer castes have a greater admixture of mediterranean and Nordic features than the others." (R. R. Diwakar: Bihar Through the Ages: PP. 78)

Another Scholar has also the same and similar view. I would like to quote

> "Aryan society, to begin with was one and undifferentiated. But the contacts with the Dravidians introduced varna or colour as the

fist mark of obvious distinction. Very soon, however that acquired a technical meaning and became a level of social differentiations. "

Aryan or Hindu society has certain fundamental features which have remained unchanged in the course of ages. Some of them have been derived from the Vedic traditions, while others have come in from other and later resources. The transformation from the Vedic into the Hindu society came about so imperceptibly that, at this distance, it is as difficult to distinguish between the original and the borrowed elements, as it is between the Aryan and the Dravidian already mentioned.

Aryans were generally vegetarians but they were not strict one. Some times they used to eat non-vegetarian diet also especially when some important guests visited them. I would like to quote here:

"Aryans were essentially vegetarians in diet, imbibing milk, ghee, clarified butter, vegetable and fruits of different varieties, and barley. On special occasions, such as the arrival of an important guest, special preparations of non-vegetarian food (meat mutton or fowl) were served, along with locally brewed wines like 'sura' or 'Madhu."(Jagdev Singh:Growth of Hindu Religion and Culture. P. 72)

According to one scholar there are traces of the division of the Aryan tribe into the 'holy power(Brahmin), the kingly power (Kstra/Kshatriya) and the commonality (Vaish/ Vaishya), and the caste system and was only in process of development in the Rig Vedic times. The kingship and priesthood was hereditary and two words (Varna and Jati) used by Sanskrit writers in one and the same sense. Varna indicated colour which meant race. Each of these major castes is again subdivided into different smaller castes and they again show that one is superior to another. For example the Vaishyas are subdivided into many castes such as Kalwar, Teli, Kanu and Sudi etc.

Thus it is clear that Hindu caste system came into vogue out of a fusion of two slightly different concepts of Varna and Jati in the beginning. Varna is certainly older term than jati according to the Rigveda.

According to K.C. Mishra Jati, which signifies birth, appears to have been a concept related with the institution of family(kula or gotra). Later, with the growth of hereditary occupational classes, both these concepts were confused and ordinarily signified what is denoted by the word Caste today. However, even in the later usages the term Varna was generally applicable to original four classes only, where as the Jati signified the numerous subdivisions of castes.

It is stated in the Vedic Indices that Hindu caste system is the product of two different concepts of varna and Jati in the beginning. Varna is in vogue since the time of the Rigveda. In the Rigveda there were only two varnas, viz. Arya and Das. Thereafter four professional classes are among Indo-Aryans.

"Jati, which signifies birth, appears to have been a concept related with the institution of family (kula or gotra). Later, with the growth of hereditary occupational classes, both these concepts were confused and ordinarily signified what is denoted by the word 'caste' (People of India) today. It has been stated that the term 'varna' was generally applicable to original four classes only, where as the Jati signified the numerous subdivisions of castes. (Manu).

Prof. Ghure, therefore, even admitting that caste in India is a Brahmanic child of Indo-Aryan culture, has shown various factors like territorial separateness, mixed origin, occupation, sectarian difference, etc. as the basis of distinction for so many subcastes, existing today.

Caste has been called'great on wall of India by many indologists and ethnologists. According to Senart, the great French indologist and ethnologist, whose authority in this respect was perhaps greater than any of his contemporaries, maintained that caste system is a normal development of ancient clan (tribal) organization of the Aryans. Sir H. Risley, the father of Indian ethnography, denied any importance of function in the origin of caste system, which in his view was a question of race and racial contrast only. Sherring attributes the multitudinous division of caste to the arrogance of the Brahmins.

One another scholar has pointed out the salient features of Aryan;

> "Aryan or indo Aryans in upperclass Hindus who are tall, fair, complexioned, sharp nosed speaking Sanskritic languages. (Suresh Chandra Banerji: Society in Ancient India P. 35).

Different scholars have defined caste differently:

> "Caste is a system in which an individual's rank and its accompanying rights and obligations are ascribed on the basis of birth into a particular group."

> According to Anderson and Parker, "Caste is that extreme form of social class organization in which the position of individual in the status hierarchy is determined by crescent and birth. "

> E.A.M. Blunt has defined caste as an endogamous or a collection of endogamous groups, bearing a common name, membership of which is hereditary; imposing on the members certain restriction in the matter of social intercourse;either following a common traditional occupation of claiming a common origin; and generally regarded as forming a single homogenous community."

According to Majumdar and Madan, 'A caste is a closed class. '

C.H. Cooley has defined caste like this:

> "When a class is somewhat strictly hereditary and whose contacts are restricted accordingly. "

> According to Lundbert Writer, "A caste is a social category whose members are assigned a permanent status within a social hierarchy and whose contacts are restricted accordingly. "

> "Caste is a system of stratification in which mobility up and down in the status ladder, at least ideally may not occur."

According to Kroeber, "Caste is an endogamous and hereditary subdivision of an ethnic unit, occupying a position of superior or inferior rank of social esteem in comparision with other subdivision."

Now a days caste is undergoing considerable changes as a consequence of urbanization, industrialization, democratization and spread of education, etc.

Caste is a hereditary, endogamous, usually localized group, having a traditional association with an occupation, and a particular position in the hierarchy of castes. Relations between castes are governed, among other things, by the concepts of pollution and purity, and generally, maximum commensality occurs within the caste (Srinivas 62-63).

1. This is important to note as, according to the common sense- definition, castes are basically endogamous and also commensal with regard to specific, purity-relevant sorts of food.
2. Jati can mean, according to the context, a caste internal status group which is not commensal with the other status groups of the same caste.
3. In some cases, jati denotes an ethnically (culturally and linguistically) distinct group which can embrace, several castes.
4. Finally, jati is used in the sense of legal status in general.

There is an aggressive ethnicisation of all social, cultural, linguistic and political issues by the various ethnic groups desinated as the Matwalis who blame it on the state for most of the wrongs in the past.

"For thirty years, the Panchayat regime made' social harmony' and 'unity in diversity' its main social and political rhetoric. The constitution of 1962 called Nepal a' multi ethnic, multi-cultural, and a multi-linguistic 'Hindu state. A Hindu ethos under the Hindu monarchy dominated the national life of Nepal during the period."

This is clear from this definition. First, membership in a caste is by birth. Second, a caste is an endogamous unit. Third, members of each caste traditionally had an occupation or trade to pursue. Fourth, castes are graded in a local hierarchy. Fifth, notions of pollution and purity govern the nature and extent of the relations between castes.

One scholar has observed that in the beginning caste had nothing to do with birth and was merely a distinction based upon qualities, character and occupation. But there can be no doubt that whatever the reasons for the origin of the system, castes soon became hereditary and more or less rigid. In the Mahabharat Yudhishtra says that Sudras possessing the qualities and virtues of a Brahmin should be treated as a Brahmin and vice versa. In the Dharmavyadha episode of the Mahabharat, a Brahmin was advised by a Brahmin lady to seek knowledge of Dharma (rightneousness) from a butcher, which he accepted that and also took food and water at the hands of his teacher.

One scholar of Mithila has defined caste in the following lines:

> "Caste was the determining factor in all aspects of social life. All important castes and groups are found in Mithila. R. K. Chaudhary:Mithila in the Age of Vidyapati: p. 119.

Socio-Cultural Traditions

Culture is like a mirror to understand a society. It is an essential basis to explain and express various characteristics of human being. Some cultural experts and sociologists have defined culture in the following lines:

According to Linton: 'Culture may be defined as the sum total of knowledge, attitudes and natural behaviour patterns shared and transmitted by the members of a particular society.

> According to Malinowsk: "Culture is the handiwork of man and the medium through which he achieved his ends.

> According to Spencer, "Culture is the super-organic environment as distinguished from the organic, or physical, the word of plants and animals.

> According to Redfield, 'Culture is an organized body of conventional understanding manifest in an art and artifact, which, persisting through tradition, characterized of Human being. '

That's why it is essential to study the life cycle of particular group for understanding various aspects of its life. Researchers are supposed to focus on its eating habits, clothing, religious practices, customs, beliefs, fairs and festivals and rites and rituals. Social customs are very binding elements to maintain and control social behaviour.

The Madheshi community celebrates birth ceremony very lavishly especially in the case of baby boy. It also observes Mundan, and marriage rites and rituals and sacred thread ceremony in a grand manner but sacred thread ceremony is not compulsory for all castes. It is mandatory for high class castes. First feeding ceremony is also not celebrated in all castes. Every caste observes its rites and rituals according to its tradition.

Pregnancy Period: This period is very precious and sensitive in the life of married women of Madheshi community because they are not looked after very attentively in lack of proper medical care especially in rural areas. Most of the women express in an interview taken by this scribe that they were looked after better at the birth of first and second child. After that they were not looked after by the members of the family and even by their spouses. They did not apply medical guidelines properly and attentively prescribed by health experts. Even they were not admitted in good health posts and hospitals meant for safe delivery. They were compelled to be pregnant by their spouses but not looked after by them at the time of delivery. They were forced to stay in their homes for delivery. So some of them even lost their lives during unsafe delivery.

Birth of any baby is essential for the balanced growth of this universe. It is also compulsory for the smooth growth of humanity. Marriage is a must for life. So when a man and woman get married, they get social licence for intercourse. This way they start sexual relations to have babies. Their congugal life begins. They get kids after some times. Their social life starts then. A mother is kept in a separate room for special care for six days. Birth pollution is observed during the period of six days. On the birth of baby child, a Chamain (Wife of Chamar) is called in and it is she who handles all rites and rituals acquired on this occasion such as delivering the baby, cutting the umbilical cord, cleaning up the blood and filth which are the byproducts because of birth and cleaning the baby and the mother. From the very day after the birth, the mother is given a broth of ginger mixed with sugar like substance called Shakhar and other spices also which is supposed to be very nutritious and potential. This is called Achhmani in local language. Till the fifth day, no rituals are performed. On the sixth day after the birth, the mother's finger and toe's nails are chopped off. She puts on sindur on her forehead. A new set of clothes is also given to put on. From this day on mother is allowed to eat rice and other eatables. Seven kinds of cereals are mixed for making a special type of nutritious diet which is called' Batisi.. It is from this day that the mother is considered purified from birth pollution. A special room is prepared for the mother which is called 'Soiri Ghar'.

Though the mother is supposed to be purified but she is not allowed to touch wells, tanks or any other water sources, even taps for a month and so on. Some castes observe this custom for only twelve days only. It varies from caste to caste of the Madheshi community. This is the tradition of some castes that if it becomes necessary for mother to bring water. then she has to first perform a ritual before she touches any water sources to get water. First of all the mother takes a water pot and places it in front of the water sources. Thereafter she has to place some rice grains, fresh green grass , and turmeric at five steps. Then worship is performed at those places and after this worship, the water of the pot is poured into the water source. After this ritual is over, she is considered pure for drawing water. Then she is supposed to serve water to any body to drink.

'During this period she is not supposed to worship or to do other household chores. On the sixth day she takes bath and also bathes the newly born baby for purification. This is called Chhathiyar ceremony. She is supposed to touch ironmade items and turmeric powder. Naming ceremony of new born baby is also done which is called Namakaran in local language. A pen is kept beside the baby. It is supposed that Vidhata (the creator) writes the fate of the baby on this auspicious occasion. Some thing auspicious is also done to ward off evil spirits.

4

Functions of the Caste System

The caste provides security to the fellow members. For instance, if a member of the caste is involved in some trouble, he is helped by the caste men.

Caste men are given a moral education regarding the customs and manners of their caste.

The caste men are deeply involved in political affairs, especially at election-time when rallies or processions occur.

The caste men are acknowledged and helped when performing sanskar such as marriage.

A genetically 'pure'line is maintained due to the caste-endogamy and clan-exogamy practiced in the caste system.

He has also pointed out defects and faults of the caste system in the following lines:

Inspite of the positive functions of castes, there are some negatives:

> The caste system sometimes creates an obstacle to national integration. The caste system also creates some problems in economic development, especially at the regional level. The caste system creates social inequality.

There was national caste hierarchy during the Rana rule. When Jang Bahadur became prime minister in 1854, the caste hierarchy was codified through the Mulki Ain. It placed castes of comparable status of the hills higher in status than similar caste groups among the Newars and the Terai Hindus. Though the Mulki Ain has forbidden the caste system but no law can break the caste hierarchy in the Madheshi society because there is division of caste since time immemorial. It is deeply rooted in it. According to one Nepali scholar R. K. R. Regmi there is social hierarchy in Nepal:

1. Hindus are superior to others.
2. Buffalo eaters are superior to beef eaters.
3. Pork eaters are inferior to buffalo eaters but are superior to beef eaters.
4. Beef eaters are the most inferior.
5. Those who eat garlic and onions are inferior to every one.
6. Those who use liquor in ritual activities are inferior than those who do not drink or eat.
7. For women, hypergamous marriage is allowed, but hypogamous marriage is not allowed.
8. They used state to intervene in matters of caste; e. g. Junga Bahadur Rana raised the caste of Salmi (Manandhar). The striking feature of caste system in Nepal is that there is no dispute about it. It is not reflected through politics.

Introduction

It was Max Mueller who introduced the word 'Arya' in 1853 into the English language referring to Aryan race and language. According to Mueller's etymological explanation 'Aryan' the word is derived from ar (to plough, to cultivate.) Four Arya Satya (Four Noble Truths). Therefore, the meaning of Arya is given as 'excellent, best, followed by respectable, and as a noun, master, lord , worthy , honourable, upholder of Aryan values. Therefore, Aryan means 'cultivator, or farmer.

There was good mingling of Aryan and Dravidian society in ancient Aryabrata. According to one Indian scholar. Aryan society, to begin with, was one and undifferentiated. But the contacts with the Dravidians introduced Varna or colour as the first mark of obvious distinction very soon, however, that acquired a technical meaning, and became a level of social differentiation.

Aryan culture is an old one. It is original in nature but in course of time it has also changed a lot. So we can say that culture is dynamic and not static S. R. Sharma has righty observed the nature of change in it. "Aryan or Hindu society has certain fundamental features which have remained unchanged in the course of ages. Some of them have been derived from the Vedic traditions, while others have come in from other and later resources.

The transformation from the Vedic to the Hindu society came about so imperceptibly that, at this distance, it is as difficult to distinguish between the original and the borrowed elements as it is between the Aryan and the Dravidian already mentioned.

Therefore, there are four divisions of Aryan society: Brahmins, Khastriya, Vaishyas and Sudras. They are called Chaturabarna or four Varnas, the tendency persisted and resulted in the ultimate creature of innumerable divisions but neither upon colour nor upon occupation but upon birth and the observance of food and marriage restrictions. There are countless castes. There is no exact and authentic date regarding this.

Nicolo Conti and Taver Nier, the Italian and French travellers of the 13th and 17th centuries respectively count 84 and 72 castes. But neither jaisi nor these travellers give correct figures of the different castes and professional class. Their subdivisions in Mughal times had become to numerous to mention.

One Indian scholar has highlighted the admixture of different castes in the following lines:

The Brahmins and the Kshatryas belong to the same racial stock, but the latter are more mixed than the former. The original

Kshatriyas lost their purity of blood by inter marriage with later Rajputs. The various artisan castes such as the Koiri, Kurmi, Kahar and Ahir, don't differ very much from each other in physical characteristics yet they represent a mixture of various racial strains. The Doms and chamars are racially even farther removed from tribal groups. Leaving aside the large hybrid elements among them the average Dom is, by modern standard, a handsomer Person than the Chamar. The incidence of hand some and attractive features among women is a cause rather that the consequence of miscogenations. The so called higher castes have a greater admixture of mediterranean and Nordic features than the others. "

Another Scholar has also the same and similar view. I would like to quote

"Aryan society, to begin with was one and undifferentiated. But the contacts with the Dravidians introduced varna or colour as the fist mark of obvious distinction. Very soon, however that acquired a technical meaning and became a level of social differentiations. "

Aryan or Hindu society has certain fundamental features which have remained unchanged in the course of ages. Some of them have been derived from the Vedic traditions, while others have come in from other and later resources. The transformation from the Vedic into the Hindu society came about so imperceptibly that, at this distance, it is as difficult to distinguish between the original and the borrowed elements, as it is between the Aryan and the Dravidian already mentioned.

Aryans were generally vegetarians but they were not strict one. Some times they used to eat non-vegetarian diet also especially when some important guests visited them. I would like to quote here:

> "Aryans were essentially vegetarians in diet, imbibing milk, ghee, clarified butter, vegetable and fruits of different varieties, and barley. On special occasions, such as the arrival of an important guest, special preparations of non-vegetarian food Meat mutton or fowl) were served,

along with locally brewed wines like 'Sura' or'Madhu.'" (Jagdev Singh: Growth of Hindu Religion and Culture. P. 72)

Thus it is clear that Hindu caste system came into vogue out of a fusion of two slightly different concepts of Varna and Jati in the beginning. Varna is certainly older term than jati according to the Rigveda.

According to K.C. Mishra Jati, which signifies birth, appears to have been a concept related with the institution of family (kula or gotra). Later, with the growth of hereditary occupational classes, both these concepts were confused and ordinarily signified what is denoted by the word Caste today. However, even in the later usages the term Varna was generally applicable to original four classes only, where as the Jati signified the numerous subdivisions of castes.

It is stated in the Vedic Index that Hindu caste system is the product of two different concepts of Varna and Jati in the beginning. Varna is in vogue since the time of the Rigveda. In the Rigveda there were only two Varnas, viz. Arya and Anarya. Thereafter four professional classes are among Indo-Aryans.

"Jati, which signifies birth, appears to have been a concept related with the institution of family (kula or gotra). Later, with the growth of hereditary occupational classes, both these concepts were confused and ordinarily signified what is denoted by the word 'caste' (People of India) today. It has been stated that the term 'varna' was generally applicable to original four classes only, where as the Jati signified the numerous subdivisions of castes. (Manu).

Prof. Ghure, therefore, even admitting that 'caste in India is a Brahmanic child of Indo-Aryan culture, has shown various factors like territorial separateness, mixed origin, occupation, sectarian difference, etc. as the basis of distinction for so many subcastes, existing today. Caste has been called'great wall of India by many indologists and ethnologists. According to Senart, the great French indologist and ethnologist, whose authority in this respect was perhaps greater than any of his contemporaries, maintained that caste system is a normal development of ancient clan (tribal) organization of the Aryans. Sir H. Risley, the father of Indian ethnography, denied any importance of function in the origin of caste system, which in his view was a question of race and racial contrast only. Sherring attributes the multitudinous division of caste to the arrogance of the Brahmins.

One another scholar has pointed out the salient features of Aryan;

> "Aryan or indo Aryans in upperclass Hindus who are tall, fair, complexioned, sharp nosed speaking Sanskritic languages.

Different scholars have defined caste differently

"Caste is a system in which an individual's rank and its accompanying rights and obligations are ascribed on the basis of birth into a particular group. "

According to Anderson and Parker, "Caste is that extreme form of social class organization in which the position of individual in the status hierarchy is determined by crescent and birth. "

E.A.M. Blunt has defined caste as an endogamous or a collection of endogamous groups, bearing a common name, membership of which is hereditary;imposing on the members certain restriction in the matter of social intercourse; either following a common traditional occupation of claiming a common origion; and generally regarded as forming a single homogenous community.

According to Majumdar and Madan, 'A caste is a closed class. 'C.H. Cooley has defined caste like this:

> "When a class is somewhat strictly hereditary and whose contacts are restricted accordingly. "

According to Lundbert Writer, "A caste is a social category whose members are assigned a permanent status within a social hierarchy and whose contacts are restricted accordingly."

"Caste is a system of stratification in which mobility up and down in the status ladder, at least ideally may not occur."

According to Kroeber, "Caste is an endogamous and hereditary subdivision of an ethnic unit, occupying a position of superior or inferior rank of social esteem in comparision with other subdivision. "

Now a days caste is undergoing considerable changes as a consequence of urbanization, industrialization, democratization, spread of education, etc.

Caste is a hereditary, endogamous, usually localized group, having a traditional association with an occupation, and a particular position in the hierarchy of castes. Relations between castes are governed, among other things, by the concepts of pollution and purity, and generally, maximum commensality occurs within the caste (Srinivas 62-63).

1. This is important to note as, according to the common sense definition, castes are basically endogamous and also commensal with regard to specific, purity-relevant sorts of food.

2. Jati can mean, according to the context, a caste internal status group which is not commensal with the other status groups of the same caste.

3. In some cases, jati denotes an ethnically (culturally and linguistically) distinct group which can embrace several castes.

4. Finally, jati is used in the sense of legal status in general.

There is an aggressive ethnicisation of all social, cultural, linguistic and political issues by the various ethnic groups desinated as the Matwalis as if, who blame it on the state for most of the wrongs in the past. "For thirty years, the Panchayat regime made' social harmony' and 'unity in diversity' its main social and political rhetoric. The constitution of 1962 called Nepal a' multi ethnic, multi-cultural, and a multilinguistic 'Hindu state.

A Hindu ethos under the Hindu monarchy dominated the national life of Nepal during the period. "

This is clear from this definition. First, membership in a caste is by birth. Second, a caste is an endogamous unit. Third, members of each caste traditionally had an occupation or trade to pursue. Fourth, castes are graded in a local hierarchy. Fifth, notions of pollution and purity govern the nature and extent of the relations between castes.

One scholar has observed that in the beginning caste had nothing to do with birth and was merely a distinction based upon qualities, character and occupation. But there can be no doubt that whatever the reasons for the origin of the system, castes soon became hereditary and more or less rigid. In the Mahabharat Yudhishtra says that Sudras possessing the qualities and virtues of a Brahmin should be treated as a Brahmin and vice versa. In the Dharmavyadha episode of the Mahabharat, a Brahmin was advised by a Brahmin lady to seek knowledge of Dharma (rightneousness) from a butcher, which he accepted that and also took food and water at the hands of his teacher.

One scholar of Mithila has defined caste in the following lines:

> "Caste was the determining factor in all aspects of social life. All important castes and groups are found in Mithila."

The Interim Constitution of Nepal recognises for the first time in Nepalese history the cultural diversity of Nepal, stating it to be a' multicaste, multi-lingual, multi-religious, multi cultural and multi-ideological nation. '

One Nepali scholar has also the same and similar view about the cultural and linguistic diversity of Nepal in the following lines:

The remarkable linguistic and social diversity in the Tarai can also pose a problem for the consolidation of a pan-Madhesi identity. Madhesis speak Maithili, Bhojpuri, and Awadhi that are also spoken across the border in India. On the other hand, ethnic groups such as the Tharus, Rajbanshi, Dhimal, and Gangai have their own languages. Similarly, the whole spectrum of the caste-based hierarchy is to be found amongst the Hindu Madhesis. Brahmins and Kshatriya groups are situated at the top, while the Dalits at the bottom are considered impure and untouchables. There is also a substantial presence of the' middle castes', like the Yadavs, Suris, and Kurmis. Caste divisions govern social relations and play a significant role in forming political choices. Very often they also shape economic stratification. (Hari Prasad Bhattarai: Recognising Diversity: P. 160).

Mishra, C. (2003), has appropriately indicated three important factors that contibuted to local isolation and involution and, thus, to the emergence and rise of multiple cultures in Nepal. (Notes on Pluralism in Nepal, Chumlung Bulletin, Vol. 2, No. 3).

The Interim Constitution of Nepal 2006 defines Nepal as a 'state which is secular, inclusive and democratic and guarantees equal and social justice.

At present one hundred and twenty five ethnic and caste groups and sub-groups, and more than one hundred languages have been documented according to the census of 2011. In addition, these caste, ethnic, and language groups are further divided into eight major religious groups:

Hindu, Buddhist, Islam, Kirat, Jain, Sikh, Christian, and Bahai. Broadly speaking, the following categories of people are to be found:

1. Pahadis: Hill and mountain groups considered caste Hindus (twice born, ascetic castes) with Nepali as their mother tounge, comprise about 39 percent of the population.

2. Janajatis: Tibeto-Burman language-speaking hill and mountain ethnic groups comprise about 22 percent.

3. Newars: Consisting of Hindus and Buddhists of different castes, comprise about five percent.

4. Madheshis: People who trace their origin to the plains comprise 32 percent. Among them about 18 percent are caste Hindus; about 10 percent are Janjatis (ethnic groups of the plains); about 4 percent Muslims; and a few other groups.

   "Madhesis are defined as non-Pahadi people who, regardless of their place of birth or residence, speak a mother tongue that belongs to the plains. However, in contemporary discourse, the category does not encompass the lowland and indigenous ethnic groups and the Muslims. Indigenous peoples like Tharus, Rajbanshis, Gangai, and Dhimals, and Muslims have claimed that they have their own independent identity that is different from that of the Madhesis. Some groups, particularly Tharus, Dhimals, and Gangais, claimed that they are the original inhabitants of the Tarai and that the Madhesis are later migrants. " But it is wrong to say that Madhesis are migrants. They are also original inhabitants of Tarai/Madhesh from time immemorial.

5. Others: Marwaris, Bengalis, Sikhs, Christians, and the 'Others' category of the census add up to about 2 persent. Thus it is right to say and support the following statement made by two emminent scholars:

The Nepali people are, in essence, a cultural mosaic compromising different castes and ethnic groups belonging to the Tibeto-Burman and Indo-Aryan linguistic families. This is indicative of the waves of migrations that have occurred over two thousand years from the north and south.

Although different groups have mingled with each other, they differ widely in cultural terms and have also adapted differently. Their sense of being different from each other, also seems to have persisted throughout history. (Pradhan, R. and A. Shrestha 2005).

According to T.R.Vaidya and B.R. Bajracharya the remarkable linguistic and social diversity in the Tarai can also pose a problem for the consolidation of a pan-Madhesi identity. Madhesis speak Maithili, Bhojpuri, and Awadhi that are also spoken across the border in India. On the other hand, ethnic groups such as the Tharus, Rajbanshi, Dhimal, and Gangai have their own languages. Similarly, the whole spectrum of the caste-based hierarchy is to be found amongst the Hindu Madhesis.

Brahmins and Kshatriya groups are situated at the top, while the Dalits at the bottom are considered impure and untouchables. There is also a substantial presence of the 'middle castes', like the Yadavas, Suris, and Kurmis. Caste divisions govern social relations and play a significant role in forming political choices. Very often they also shape economic stratification. (Hari Prasad Bhattarai: Cultural Diversity. P. 160)

There are many castes and cultures in Terai–Madhesh.

According to one scholar;

> "The word Tarai is derived from Persian language which means humid or muggy land. The Tarai plains stretch the length of the Southern Border and are home to half the total population including many non-Madhesh (both indigenous ethnic groups and recent migrants from the hill.)"

Terai is also called Madhesh now a days because Madheshi people do not face identity crisis. The interim constitution has also recognized it. The historical two Madheshi movements have also focused on it to a great extent. Consequently Madhesh has its own monograms and testimony. Nobody can deny its existence in the true sense of the term. One Madheshi scholar has identified Madhesh in the following lines. Madheshi scholar like C. K. Lal has asserted that the term' Madhesh' refers to the cultural space where Madheshis reside. He said he preferred the term 'Madhesh'to Terai Bȧsi because the word Terai carries the connotation of internal colonization. (2005).

Madhesh refers to the terai region specific to Nepal, approximate 23 to 35 wide broad belt of alluvial and fertile land stretching from Mahakali river in the west to Mechi river in the east between Indian border in the south and Sivaliks/Chure range in the north. Etymologically, Madhesh has been claimed to be derived from word Madhyadesh (mid country) or Matsyadesh (fish country) whose capital is said to be in Biratnagar. With the evolution along time, along with its historic values and usages, the word Madhesh has acquired cultural aspects into it that today it represents a way of life and different aspects of life -styles of people living specifically in the region. Whether is Madheshi- Haat or Madheshi-colour, whether it is Madheshi cuisines or Madheshi'boli-byabahar', the word has integrated different cultural aspects into it, and thus stands with a cultural connotations." Vivaswan Kumar: Madhesh or Terai and Tharus or Madheshis: New Frontiers of Etymopolitics in Nepal: March 4, 2007.

Madhesh literary means mid- century (Middle country). It is Madhyadesh in Hindi. Madhese and Madheshi are two different words. First is derogatory where where as the second one is acceptable to the all Madheshi people. Madhesh is an offensive marker of humiliation of the Madheshi Citizens in terms of geography and their colour. Madhesh is immensely marginalized in the polity and governance of the nation. It is still politically under represented. It is stepmotherly behaved by the Nation. The language and culture of the Madheshi people is not equally treated by the ruler elites. There has been a long tradition of discrimination and exclusion. There is also huge psychological division between Madhesh and Mountain since a long time. This type of division is not healthy for the sound health of the nation. Madhesh is a bread basket of Nepal. It covers the 17percent of the territory of the whole country. It is also home of more than 40 percent people. It is a major source of national revenue and also centre of economic activities. The progress of the nation depends upon the progress of Madhesh in the true sense of the term. It is very important to address the main problems of Madhesh and the Madheshi people. It is also very necessary to fulfill their aspirations for the long term stability of democratic process, sustainable peace and progress in Nepal. Upendra Yadav has positive view regarding Terai/ Madhesh. I would like to quote him here:

"The Madhesh is the most important region of the Nepal, geographically and culturally distinct from the hills. However, the terai region or the Madhesh of Nepal, could attract comparatively little attention of foreign scholars because it is hot, dusty and malarious. Consequently, little interest was taken about the Terai's geographical, historical, economical or cultural characteristics, despite the fact that it comprises 21 percent Nepal's land area which inhabits more than 50 percent of Nepali population. This neglect is striking, because the Madhesh is the backbone of Nepal's economy, producing about 65 per cent of the nations gross domestic product (GDP) yielding about 76 percent of the governments revenue, and 60 percent agricultural products of the country. " (Upendra Yadav 2005, P. 18-19.).

Cheah (2008) says, "Madhesh not only implies a physical composition of the space that stretches across the southern belt of Nepal, but also includes the cultural and lingual space that exists as a basis of identity amongst many people residing in the region. "Similarly, the pioneer researcher and scholar on Madhesh, Gaige (1975) defined Madheshi people as those who speak plains' languages as their mother tongue or first language, whether they were born or live in the plains or hills. Bhattachan (2008) says (cited in Yadav, 1997),

"Madhesh is a historical, political and sociological concept that refers to a group or communities discriminated by the dominant groups where as Teraibasi refers to any caste or ethnic group, including the dominant caste or group. "

Gaige and Hachhethu (2007) also define Madhesh as a plain landscape from Siwalik Hill range and the term Madheshi broadly encompass people of non-hill origin; their cultural identity is specially associated with the Hindu castes (from the plains) of Maithili and Bhojpuri speaking populations.

The Madheshi community is composed of the traditional Hindu caste hierarchy such as Brahaman, Kshatriya, Baisya and Dalits, and indigenous peoples, other native tribes and Muslims. Madhesh, one of the three ecological zones of Nepal, covers 23 percent of the total land area and is 800 kilometers with its width varying from 25 to 32 kms. The boundary of Madhesh starts from the foothills of the Siwalik or Churia range of the Himalayas in the north and extends up to the Indian border in the south. Out of the 75 districts in Nepal, 20 districts, namely Jhapa, Morang, Sunsari, Saptari, Siraha, Dhanusha, Mahottari, Sarlahi, Rautahat, Bara, Parsa, Chitwan, Nawalparasi, Rupandehi, Kapilvastu, Dang. Banke, Bardiya, Kailali and Kanchanpur have been known as Madhesh (Jha, 2011). The total population of Madhesh constitutes 49.3 percent of the entire population of Nepal, making it the most densely populated region of the Nation. (C.B.C. 2O11).

The residents of Madhesh can be categorised into Madheshi and Pahadi or hill communities. Madheshi people have been living in Madhesh for centuries with their own distinct language and dialects, unique pattern of dreaming and traditions where as the hill people are of hill origin and they came to Madhesh during the course of migration. Their tradition, culture and rituals are different from those of the Madheshi communities. (The Landscape of Madhesh. P. 118.).

Dilli Ram Dahal's opinion is also quotable here:

> "By ethnic/caste groups, tarai encompasses the diverse cultural groups ranging from the hill origin (the hill origin caste groups, Adibasi/ Janajati and Dalits) to the tarai-origin peoples or Madhesi (caste origin groups including tarai dalits, Adibasi/ Janjati groups and others. In brief, the tarai today presents a distinct multi-cultural region or the' melting pot' in terms of settlement of various groups of people.

No systematic and scientific study has been made so far in this field. The detailed ethnographic studies of the Madhesh community are limited. According to sociologist Dilli Ram Dahal:

There is little disaggregated socioeconomic data on various groups of people of Nepal even today. In brief, little is known about the people of the Tarai even today, particularly the 'Madheshi people, with reference to their origin, history, culture, socioeconomic conditions and the processes of inclusion/ exclusion among them." (Dahal 2013).

One of the most neglected areas of social science research in Nepal is the Tarai, a strip of tropical flat land, occupying 20 districts, where 50.15 percent of the total population of Nepal lives today (C.B.S. 2011).

So, there is an urgent need of anthropological and sociological study of these castes. Every caste has its glorious history of its origin but there is no proper study is done in this regard. Every caste has religious history of its origin.

Only two of the origin tales texts are available so far they are Chitragupta Katha and Shri Chanwar Puran. Others have oral tradition to tale their origin tales. Very recently Deepak Chaudhary has wriitten a small book about Dev caste of Terai Madhesh which is his M.A. dissertation. Ram Narayan Dev has also added a volume to the study of Dev caste. Thus Dev caste has attracted the attention of the research scholars.

Previous studies: First of all Dor Bahadur Bista has written a book named' People of Nepal' on the basis of his field study which has proved a mile stone in this regard. F. H. Gaige (1975) has raised the Madheshi's burning issues very seriously and scholarly manner. Thereafter Rishi keshavraj Regmi has also written a book. Upendra Yadav 's book named Conspiracy against Madhesh is very thought-provoking. J. P. Gupta's some books in Nepali Vernacular are also worth reading. Makhan Jha (1971) in his book The Sacred Complex of Janakpur' has tried his level best to explore various aspects of Janakpur 's religious complex. A British scholar Richard Burgahrt (1978) has also concentrated on the Maithili culture and civilisation. This is a part of his PhD dissertation. Meena Acharya (1981) in her research work 'The Maithili women of Sirisa has focussed on the social, cultural and economic conditions of the women folk of the Mithila region in details. This is the first and last work done about the life style of Maithili women. Haribansh Jha (1993) has highlighted Madheshi's multiple problems in his book 'Tarai Community and National Integration in Nepal'.

Deepak Chaudhary has written a good book named Tarai/ Madhesh of Nepal in which he has dealt with many major castes of Tarai/Madhesh. This scribe has also written two books on Madhesh' Janakpur, the Sacred Jewel of Nepal' and' Murder of Madhesh'. Kalyan Bhakta Mathema is a writer of Madhesh Uprising and there is a latest book on Madhesh named' The Landscape of Madhesh' edited by Ruhi Tewari and Anirudh Prasad Sah. Besides, some books have been written in Nepali language also on Madhesh and Madheshi movements. Two Madheshi movements have inspired and motivated some Madheshi writers to write and think about Madheshi sentiments and sensibilities. Now they write in Hindi, Maithili, Bhojpuri, Awadhi and Bajjika in ever genre of their literature vigoriously but they are getting no incentives from the Nepal government. Recently the Culture Ministry of Nepal has started Vidyapati Kosh (treasury) to inspire and encourage the Maithili writers. It has also awarded some imminent writers for their outstanding works. This is a good start and it will be appreciated by every one.

But it matters little that Terai/ Madheshi scholars and thinkers have contributed substancially to the production of knowledge or that they have expressed their finest sensibilities in creative arts, architecture, poetry and literature. It is a matter of great regret that they have not been evaluated properly and intellectually. They have been behaved stepmotherly in each and every field of life. They are considered as second class writers and thinkers. In Republic Nepal the politicization of community identities draws historical traditions and perceptions. My own writings unfold the enchanting ethnic diversity of Madheshi communities and the variety in their social and cultural traits and engage with identity and representional issues and their relevance to the rise of Madheshi nationalism. "Caste prejudice in India is still very strong and ingrained and changes for the better can only be effected slowly. These castes form the majority of India's landless labour and they will have to be provided with land if their economic status is to be improved. "The same and similar condition is prevailing in Nepal also especially in Terai/ Madhesh. (Religion and Communities of India: P. 122).

References

1. Arjun Guneratne: Many Tongues one People: Cornell University Press, 1961.
2. Arjun Guneratne: The Tarai History Society, Environment: ANHS Himal Books, 2011.
3. N. K. Bhandari: Cultural Heritage of India: Aavishkar Publishers; Jaipur; 2003.
4. Punam Kumari: Social and Cultural Life of the Nepalese: Mohit Publications: New Delhi" 1999.
5. Rajesh Gautam: Rajbanshi of Nepal: Adroit Publishers. New Delhi. 2005.
6. Ram Dayal Rakesh: Janakpur: The Sacred Jewel of Nepal: Safari Nepal Publications: 2005.
7. Sabita Sapkota: Nepalese History and Culture: Himalaya Book Stall: . Kathmandu. 2004.
8. Sushil K. Naidu: Nepalese Society and Culture: Kalinga Publishers: New Delhi 1999.
9. Deepak Chaudhary: Tarai/Madhesh of Nepal: Ratna Pustak Bhandar: Kathmandu, 2013.
10. Prakash Upadhyay: Nepali Culture and Society: Kshitiz Prakashan, Kirtipur, 2012.
11. Sameera Maiti: The Tharu: Their Arts and Crafts: Northern Book Centre, New Delhi, 2004.
12. Giriraj Shah: Glory of Indian Culture: Diamond Pocket Books, New Delhi, 2003.
13. K.S. Singh: The Scheduled Castes (Revised Edition) Oxford India Paperbacks: Oxford University Press, 2010.
14. Trans. Dilip Chitre: Says Tuka: Penguin Books. New Delhi, 1991.

CONCLUSION

A republican modern Nepal is bound to follow a secular policy which could considerably reduce the suspicion of other non Hindu communities and castes. The needs to frame and formulate national policies relating to minority languages and culture, secure their fundamental and human rights and laydown a democratic and equitable basis for power to ethnic minorities. Nepal is a rainbow country. She is a golden garden of different flowers of different colours.

So how to tend this garden P.R. Sharma writes:

> All conflict prone situations would be resolved by taking recourse to dialogue between the contendng parties, without sacrificing the long-term interests of national integration.

According to Fareed Jakaria democracy is the best form of government though it has many drawbacks and demerits. So the role of political parties in elected parliament is to work for maintaining communal harmony. It requires that they should safeguard the democratic values both in letter and spirit, by relying on the institutional process rather than on personal and adhoc policies.

As an 'ethnic turntable of Asia, Nepal is a multinational multilingual, multireligious and multicultural society. The population of Nepal is about three crores of them 125 different language groups have been identified with thousands of dialect speakers. Hinduism, Buddhism and Animism are popularly known religions of Nepal.

Hahan remarks, modernization increases levels of competition for jobs, housing and other valued resources among ethnic groups and that ethnic conflict and social movements based on ethnic boundaries (rather than some other) occur when ethnic competition increases.

Coping to South Asia ethnic based policies seems to be a regular phenomenon. Perils of prosperity on the one hand, and economic backwardness on the other hand resilience, ethnocists however, point to, a decline trend of institution building the current constitutional arrangement is being maneouvered for more concentration of power in the lands of the ruling elite at the centre, treating the states as a beggars at the door. So this should not be done in Nepal because it is also going to be a federal state in near future.

Diamond remarks, ethnic conflict has polarized the policy, embittered all groups, and provided an excuse for increasingly authoritarian measures.

Brass remarks, "ethnic groups as the social force use ethnicity to make concrete demands, to alter their status, and to improve significant political power in society. I am bound to quote:

"If ethnic problems are not successfully contained ethnic divisions are enduring persistent and emotional, and they contain high prospereity for outbursts of voilence states'-- Manzy

Varna and caste have now outlined their utility. It is time when we should recast our social structure on the basis of complete equality. History has proved that man is a highly individualistic and group mined creature who apt to divide and separate even where perfect unity and equality is intended. a concept or a system based on a view to divide may only aggravate the division. Man's natural separatism should not be assisted by social separatism, it should rather be fought by social equlaism, at all levels and at all points:-- Gokulesh Sharma.

Not only that but the case system, despite their glaring

drawbacks, did play a vary significant part in maintaining the purity and solidarity of Hindu Society at the time of extenral aggressions and alien rule. According to these scholars, who includes Dr. Suniti K Chatterji it was te caste system of Hindus that saved their culture from the onslaughts of Islam and Christianity and kept undefiled the original current.

I would like to quote again:

> "A certain section of scholars maintains that the concept of four fold varnas was really a novel and useful device of the Hindu sociological brain to maintain the purity and solidarity of the society but later on what caused the decay and disintegration of society was not the Varna classification but its gradual degeneration into innumerable castes and subcastes."

According to him the quintessence of the Varna Dharma:

1. Unchangeable inequality based on birth
2. classification of occupations and their disparity
3. Prohibition of marriage outside one's own Varna.

As regards the age of the bride, the general rule is that she must be younger than the groom. But, the exact age is a matter of controversy.

I. One whose menstural flow is imminent, i.e. who is first for sexual union.

II. One who has not attained womanhood and has not experienced the impulse of youth

III. One whose looks beautiful without dress.

IV One whose menstural flow has not yet commenced and whose breasts are not yet developed. Suresh Chandra Banerjee-- Society in Ancient India, p.35.

The Interim Constitution of Nepal 2006 defines Nepal as a 'State which is secular, inclusive and democratic and gurantees equal and social justice. One French scholar has also accepted that there is heirarchy in Nepalese society. There is feeling of pure and polluted, gender unequality and it determines social relation in soiety. This is also equally true in the Madheshi society. I would like to quote:

> "The idea behind hierachy, purity and pollutron. the conceptualization of gender inquality, the stress on communality, all symbolically meaningful factors, convey the meaning to the actions undertaken by social agents and to mechanism enforcing social relations." Gerard Toffin (2008).

So it is quite clear that there is still strong caste system prevalent in the Madheshi society though some barriers have been broken. Now there is love marriage taking place in the society. Intercaste marriage is also in vogue. Living together relationship is also growing day by day. Let us hope that one day this caste system will disappear and there will be casteles and classless society in Terai Madhesh.

INDEX